THE
WISDOM
OF
ANXIETY

THE
WISDOM
OF
ANXIETY

How Worry & Intrusive Thoughts Are Gifts to Help You Heal

SHERYL PAUL

sounds true
BOULDER, COLORADO

Sounds True
Boulder, CO 80306

This book is not intended as a substitute for the medical recommendations of
physicians, mental health professionals, or other health-care providers. Rather, it is
intended to offer information to help the reader cooperate with physicians, mental
health professionals, and health-care providers in a mutual quest for optimal well-
being. We advise readers to carefully review and understand the ideas presented
and to seek the advice of a qualified professional before attempting to use them.

Published 2019

Cover design by Lisa Kerans
Book design by Beth Skelley

The section "Alcohol and Anxiety" (pp. 113–15) was original published in
"The No. 1 Change That Could Reduce Anxiety (That Almost No One Tries),"
MindBodyGreen, https://www.mindbodygreen.com/0-15748/the-1-change-that-
could-reduce-anxiety-that-almost-no-one-tries.html. Reprinted with permission
from MindBodyGreen.

Printed in the United States of America

Library of Congress Cataloging-in-Publication Data

Names: Paul, Sheryl, 1971- author.
Title: The wisdom of anxiety : how worry and intrusive thoughts are gifts to
  help you heal / Sheryl Paul.
Description: Boulder, CO : Sounds True, Inc., [2019]
Identifiers: LCCN 2018046519 (print) | LCCN 2018055592 (ebook) |
  ISBN 9781683643364 (ebook) | ISBN 9781683642503 (pbk.)
Subjects: LCSH: Anxiety.
Classification: LCC BF575.A6 (ebook) | LCC BF575.A6 P38 2019 (print) |
  DDC 152.4/6—dc23
LC record available at https://lccn.loc.gov/2018046519

To my family—Daev, Everest, and Asher—three
beautiful, sensitive souls who bring rivers of love,
kindness, meaning, and joy into my life every day

Jung observed that most of the neurosis, the feeling
of fragmentation, the vacuum of meaning, in modern
lives, results from this isolation of the ego-mind from
the unconscious. . . . If we try to ignore the inner world,
as most of us do, the unconscious will find its way
into our lives through pathology: our psychosomatic
symptoms, compulsions, depressions, and neuroses.

ROBERT JOHNSON
Inner Work: Using Dreams and Active Imagination for Personal Growth

CONTENTS

PRACTICES

ANXIETY IS A DOORWAY

> Carl Jung said that if you find the psychic wound
> in an individual or a people, there you also find
> their path to consciousness. For it is in the heal-
> ing of our psychic wounds that we come to know
> ourselves. . . . In the evolution of consciousness, our
> greatest problem is always our richest opportunity.
>
> **ROBERT JOHNSON**
> *We: Understanding the Psychology of Romantic Love*

Anxiety is the wound of our times. According to the World Health Organization, 260 million people are diagnosed with anxiety worldwide—and millions more are without a diagnosis. These numbers clearly indicate that we are living in an age of anxiety. This profound psychic wound crosses all boundaries by which we typically classify ourselves, for anxiety, like loss, is one of the great equalizers: it doesn't matter how old you are, where you live, what you look like, how much money you make, your sexual orientation, or your gender—eventually everyone will meet anxiety in the dark of night.

While the nature of the wound is clear, what is less clear from a mainstream perspective is how to address it. Guided by a Western mindset that seeks to erase pain in all forms (physical, emotional, mental, and spiritual), most people see anxiety and its cohort of symptoms as something to hide, deny, distract from, or eradicate. What we don't realize is that when we regard anxiety only as a problem and seek to eliminate the symptoms, it is pushed underground, where it's forced to rise back up with greater intensity, and we also miss the rich opportunity to evolve both individual and cultural consciousness that anxiety invites.

For anxiety is both the wound and the messenger, and at the core of the message is an invitation to wake up. In order to decipher the specifics of its messages, we have to shift from a mindset of shame, which sees anxiety as evidence of brokenness, to a mindset of curiosity, which recognizes that anxiety is evidence of our sensitive heart, our imaginative mind, and our soul's desire to grow toward wholeness. Anxiety, when approached from the mindset of learning, directs you to something deep inside that needs to be seen, a call from soul to pay attention, an invitation from the wellsprings of being to turn inward and heal at the next layer of growth.

One element that reduces the shame around anxiety is knowing that you're not alone; normalization causes shame to shrink. From the cross section of my worldwide audience, I hear the same symptoms and thoughts: "What if I married the wrong person?" "What if I have a terminal illness?" "What if I run out of money?" "What if something horrible happens to someone I love?" "What if I hurt my baby?" These are all clues that anxiety is the wound of our times and that we're in the territory of the collective unconscious. Carl Jung coined the term "collective unconscious" to describe the part of the mind that is common to all humans; and these thoughts, emerging from a shared psyche, point to the archetypal themes and stories where anxiety constellates: relationships, health, money, parenthood, the need for safety and security. Over the years, clients have shared these thoughts in hushed tones, but because I write about them weekly on my blog, they know that they're not alone. One of the blessings of the internet is that the contents of the collective unconscious, formerly only accessible via dreams and myths, are now more widely accessible. You are far from alone with your anxiety, no matter how it manifests.

Anxiety's emissaries arrive in many forms: worry, intrusive thoughts, obsessions, compulsions, insomnia, somatic symptoms. If we greet these emissaries with shame and try to sequester them into the far down, hidden recesses of psyche, they will gather in numbers and strength until we are forced to listen. As they scream for attention, the culturally induced, shaming voices take over and say, "You're broken. You're fundamentally wrong. These thoughts and symptoms are evidence that there's something deeply, pathologically wrong with you. Don't talk about. Don't admit it. Try to get rid of it as quickly and cleanly as possible."

Seeing anxiety and intrusive thoughts as wise manifestations of the unconscious is a vastly different view—and a much more hopeful and life-enhancing view—of anxiety than the one our culture holds. For what I've witnessed over the last twenty years of working closely in the underworld of psyche is that when we turn toward our symptoms instead of medicalizing and pathologizing them, we begin to gather our gold. Anxiety is a doorway into a self that longs for wholeness. Our symptoms, when honored, lead the way. When you meet your darkest, most uncomfortable places with a mindset of curiosity and compassion, you transform, and your life expands in untold ways. I've seen it countless times with my clients, my course members, my friends, my children, and in my own life. The same can be true for you.

Brazil: My Initiation into Anxiety

There were several pivotal events in my life that invited me to realign with my soul, times when my inner self grabbed me by the ankles and dragged me into the underworld. The first, and most powerful, was a panic attack that broke me open when I was twenty-one, a few months before I graduated from college. It was that panic attack and the subsequent years of drowning in daily anxiety that shattered my illusion of my "perfect life." It destroyed my glass castle of superiority, the belief that I was beyond suffering, created and confirmed by years of immersion in an education system that rewarded me for being school-smart. It destroyed my conviction that I had the right answers, or any answers. In short, it brought me to my knees in all ways—from heart palpitations to a phobia of driving that ensued after that first panic attack to night terrors and nightmares that punctuated my sleep for years. And yet, from the ashes, the pain, and the total destruction of life as I had known it, a new life—and a life's work—was born. This is how our unconscious, working through anxiety and its sisterhood of symptoms, invites us toward wholeness: we're broken open, brought to our knees, dragged into the underworld *not* to be tortured or because there's something wrong or disordered with us, but because there's something right and beautiful inside that is longing to be seen and known.

The seeds of my panic attack had been planted a year before and were intimately connected to a trip to Brazil my junior year of college. I never planned to go to Brazil. Having spoken Spanish throughout high school and into college, I had always planned to travel to Spain. But then the Brazil bug bit me: I had taken a Brazilian dance class the summer after my first year of college, and I was hooked by the dance and the culture. I danced all summer. I danced through the next year and immersed myself in Brazilian music. Quite impulsively, I changed my plans and set into motion an experience that would alter the course of my life.

In January 1990, instead of getting on a plane to Spain, I headed for Salvador, Brazil, where I was immediately pummeled when the fantasy I had built up in my mind clashed hard with the reality I encountered. In a single moment, I was yanked from my safe, clean, upper-middle-class life and hammered down into the middle of a life I had never known on any level. I lived in *favelas* where cockroaches the size of snails lined the floors and ceilings in such numbers that white paint seemed black; I witnessed a man get shot during Carnival; I daily walked past pools of fresh blood on the streets; I nearly drowned in a sudden riptide; I had trouble finding anything healthier than Guaraná to drink (basically sugar water). For months, I ate what I thought were crushed peanut cakes from vendors on the side of the road only to learn at the end of the trip that they were actually crushed shrimp cakes that had been sitting in the hot sun all day. All my systems, from the physical to the spiritual, were on high-alert overload.

Those four months terrified me, yet they were also what initiated me into an essential breakdown that would lead to following the bread crumbs of anxiety and panic into my true self. Some people are initiated through ancient rites in the middle of a forest. Some people are initiated through a crisis of health, relationship, or faith. I was initiated in Brazil. And when I look back now, I can clearly see that I was pulled to Brazil by invisible forces: the dance, the music—something unnamable led me there. It was out of character for me to be so impulsive, but nothing was going to stop me; I had to go. I had to be broken open. The story of my life as I had known it—that I was somehow above suffering—had to shatter so that the underworld of hidden pain that lived inside the polished persona could emerge and be healed.

We're all offered experiences that break us open to our core. One of the fatal flaws of our culture is that we take everything at face value and fail to see the metaphor, which, itself, contains the keys to healing. When a client comes to me convinced that he has cancer, regardless of the fact that he received a clean bill of health the week before, it takes time to quiet the ego's convincing story enough to explore the deeper underpinnings that are longing to be known. If we remain attached to addressing the anxiety at the level of the story—which usually looks like seeking endless reassurance—we'll remain stuck in anxiety. But if we can crack open the story and see that the fear of cancer, for example, is pointing to a need to develop tolerance for uncertainty and explore the metaphor that something is "eating away" at one's heart or soul, shifts begin to occur.

In my story, Brazil wasn't the problem. In fact, it took me years to understand that Brazil was the screen onto which my own unworked shadow—the pain, fear, and trauma that had to be shoved down in my first twenty years in order to keep going—was projected. Because Brazil carried my shadow, I couldn't see its beauty; I only saw the terror and despair that lived inside of me reflected in my surroundings. And it took having a panic attack while driving down the 405 freeway in Los Angeles for the shadow to rise to the surface where I could finally see it, work with it, and heal.

The ensuing years, which were the decade of my twenties, were both painful and transformative. In my early twenties, I entered a graduate program in depth psychology, which helped me begin to make sense of my anxiety through the lens of Jungian theory, which understands that symptoms are messengers from the unconscious, inviting us to grow toward wholeness. In my midtwenties, after working with a series of mediocre therapists, I landed on the couch of a brilliant man who guided me through the terrain of anxiety and helped me navigate my inner landscape. I read voraciously about transitions and wrote my first book, *The Conscious Bride*, which explores the underbelly of the wedding rite of passage. I began to work with clients struggling through their own transitions, especially around relationships, and helped them understand the invitations and metaphors embedded in their presenting stories.

None of this would have happened without Brazil. For years I regretted that experience, until eventually I realized that Brazil was my soul's way of forcing me to grow. It wasn't an accident; and your life isn't an accident either—not your anxiety, your wounds, your failures, or your traumas. In fact, the great sages teach that the seed for healing lives at the center of each trauma, meaning that your greatest challenge will also be your greatest strength. When I look back on Brazil, I know that it was through that experience that my inner world demanded to be known. Anxiety and panic were the doorways that led me to peel away the layers of pain and adapted persona that needed to be shed so that I could live closer to my true self. Anxiety is your doorway, too.

A Road Map Through Anxiety

This book will guide you step-by-step through the necessary mindsets and tools that will help you transform your relationship to anxiety so that you can release yourself from its grip and learn to decode its messages.

In part 1, I will clearly define anxiety and its symptoms as well as articulate the origins and causes of anxiety. I discuss the three pillars that allow the sensitive soul—and what I've come to see over the years of working with thousands of people is that we are all, to varying degrees, sensitive souls—to navigate successfully through life: understanding who you are and how you're wired, understanding how transitions are crucial breaking and renewal points that can either calcify or heal layers of anxiety, and offering the foundational keys of curiosity, compassion, stillness, and personal responsibility, which allow you to transform anxiety from a burden to a gift. I will also discuss the most challenging roadblock that appears anytime we set out in the direction of healing: resistance.

In part 2, I will guide you through the four realms of self—body, thoughts, emotions, and soul—so that you can learn to decipher the messages embedded in each realm. My work is holistically based, which means that, while most approaches address anxiety from a physical (somatic healing), emotional/psychological (some talk therapy), or cognitive (behavioral therapy and most talk therapies) perspective, my work encompasses all three of these areas plus a fourth: our soul. As I view anxiety not as something to get rid of but as a call for healing, part 2 will help you understand that anxiety is a messenger that is pointing to unmet needs and unhealed places in all four realms.

In part 3, I will explore how anxiety shows up in your intimate relationships with friends, partners, and children. Because our culture sends the erroneous message that fear and love are mutually exclusive and doesn't understand the paradoxical nature of love in all forms, when anxiety appears in our relationships, it's easy to believe that there's something wrong. This section explodes that belief and replaces it with a model that supports healthy love and mindful parenting so that we don't allow shame and anxiety to tear at the fabric of our most sacred and meaningful relationships.

In each section, I'll share stories both from my clients' experiences and moments of my own life that highlight how to sink below the surface of anxiety and tap into the wellsprings of wisdom that it offers. These stories will teach in a spiral as opposed to a linear fashion, meaning I'll write about tending to grief in the chapter on transitions and reference back to transitions when talking about grief. Despite what the culture teaches, learning isn't linear, but follows the circular, spiral rhythm of the soul. This book, while organized into chapters, follows the soul rhythm as well.

Throughout the book, I'll be offering both on-the-spot practices and deep-dive practices for healing from anxiety. On-the-spot practices are actions you can take in the moment, anywhere, at any time: in a meeting, on the elevator, in the airplane, at a party, in bed at night. They won't heal the anxiety from the root, but they'll help you move through a high-anxiety moment and will also help you take anxiety a few notches down in general so that you can engage in the deeper practices.

The deep-dive practices are those that will heal anxiety from the ground up and help you decipher its messages. These are practices that I'll be encouraging you to engage with every day, preferably when you first wake up in the morning (before you grab your phone) and at night before you go to sleep. As you read through the pages of this book, you will glean a lot of information about the roots of your anxiety, and this information will likely translate into personal insight. Write down these aha moments as they arise, either in the margins of this book or in a journal. Then use these insights as springboards from which to engage regularly with the deep-dive practices. Insight is essential, but it's action that metabolizes the insight into your body and heart and result in change. It's a simple formula: insight + action = change. If you want to break free from anxiety, practice is key.

While all the tools are designed to be practiced on your own, inner work is infinitely more effective when we're witnessed and guided by a skilled professional. As such, if you're not currently in therapy, I recommend finding a therapist who can work alongside you on this journey. Throughout history, humans have sought counsel from mentors and shamans, religious figures and teachers, and for many modern people, therapists fill those roles. *We are not meant to figure life out on our own.* Also, don't hesitate to share this book with your therapist. While they will have their own model and mindset from which they work, good therapists will always be open to learning new philosophies and tools that might help their clients, and possibly even themselves, grow and heal.

Key Terms on the Journey

In order to decipher anxiety's messages, it's helpful to understand the primary vessels through which anxiety communicates, so I'll define here the terms that you'll be encountering throughout this book.

Soul. Our guiding principle. Jungian theorists refer to the soul as the Self with a capital S, and it is another word for the unconscious. We connect most deeply with this aspect of ourselves through dreams and symptoms, and it's this inner guide that presents the symptoms that we'll be discussing throughout this book—anxiety, rumination, worry, intrusive thoughts, insomnia—as it attempts to bring us back into alignment with our core essence. Psyche, another term you'll find in this book, is another word for soul. In fact, in Greek mythology, Psyche is the goddess of the soul.

Spirit. The connecting energy or source that is both inside each of us and beyond us. We connect to spirit most often through creativity, imagination, nature, meditation, the arts, animals, and prayer. We feel spirit at the birth of a child, at weddings, while standing at the base of giant redwoods or on the shores of the ocean. Some people connect to spirit in a religious context, but many people connect to this animating principle in ways that have nothing to do with organized religion. Joseph Campbell describes it as "the generating energy of the life that is within you and all things." In its simplest definition, spirit is interchangeable with love.

Ego. The ego, which simply means "I" in Latin, is the part of ourselves that is conscious and of which we are aware. As Robert Johnson writes in *Inner Work*,

> When we say "I" we are referring to only that small sector of ourselves of which we are aware. We assume that "I" contains only *this* personality, *these* traits, *these* values and viewpoints that are up on the surface within the ego's range of vision, accessible to consciousness. This is my limited, highly inaccurate version of who "I" am.

The ego is our conscious self and is a necessary and healthy part of our psychological structure, but it also includes the fear-based parts of our personality. The ego includes our conscious aspects—both the ability to think, feel, reflect, plan, and execute, and the part of us that feels so comfortable with what we know (conscious awareness) that it resists the unknown realm of the unconscious. When we believe that we are *only* our conscious/ego selves, we lose touch with the guiding principle of our lives, which is our soul/unconscious.

Resistance. Ego has many subsets, including resistance, which is the part of us that is scared to grow because it fears change. Resistance clings to the status quo and often shows up as laziness, inertia, numbness, and fear. In order to gather the gifts of anxiety and grow to our next level of consciousness, we have to work actively with resistance so that it doesn't run the show. The paradox of the ego is that it both resists growth and longs to be in relationship to the soul. Part of the tension of being human is being in relationship with this paradox.

Individuation. Robert Johnson explains in *Inner Work* that "*individuation* is the term Jung used to refer to the lifelong process of becoming the complete human beings we were born to be. Individuation is our waking up to our total selves." The process of individuating includes shedding aspects of the conditioned personalities that we absorbed through the process of growing up but that are not in alignment with our true selves.

For example, if a child grows up to become a doctor to please her parents, but deep inside her passion lies in animal communication, when she's broken open through anxiety or during a transition, she will have been invited to shed at least one layer of the need to please her parents, which will allow her to come closer to her true self. Every time we walk through a transition consciously, as we'll see later in the book, we have an opportunity to shed a layer of our conditioned

mindsets, habits, beliefs, and intergenerational patterns that
no longer serve us. Anxiety and its attending feelings that arise
during transitions and at other times in life are the arrows
that point the way along the journey of individuating.

Anxiety is the bridge that connects ego to soul, conscious to unconscious, and when we learn how to harness the wisdom of anxiety, the richness and messages contained in the unconscious can inform and expand our conscious lives.

A Call to Grow

Anxiety asks you, dear reader, to embrace the gift of who you are. Maybe you've been told that you're too much—too sensitive, too dramatic, too emotional, too analytical—and this message was translated inside your young self to mean that you were wrong or broken in some way. But you must begin to know now, as hopefully you will as you read through this book, that there's absolutely nothing wrong with you. You're not broken. You're not too much. You're not wrong. In fact, it's the very qualities that you've been shamed for that you now need to wrap up like a hurt animal and hug close to your heart. For it's when you stop seeing your sensitivity as a burden and instead recognize it as the gift it is that you will begin to heal the hurt places inside you and bring your full presence into the world.

The self-protective habit you've learned is to ignore the anxiety at best and judge it at worst. Bereft of tools that teach you to move toward your discomfort and encouraged by a culture that is externally oriented—where your self-worth is correlated to external factors like appearance, career status, financial assets, and achievements—you've developed an ingrained habit to track outward toward anything that will distract from or numb the pain. You may reach for external addictions like a digital device, a shopping spree, a drug, or staying busy through Googling, Facebooking, working, advancing, climbing the ladder, or to internal distractions like worry and intrusive thoughts. You so desperately want to avoid the "fundamental groundlessness of being," as Pema Chödrön refers to a basic aspect of being human that feels out of control as it knows that our lives are informed by constant change and loss. The groundlessness is the sadness you feel around the passage of time, knowing that life is always in transition. The groundlessness is the fear of big feelings since nobody taught you how to tend to them with kindness. The groundlessness is the nameless fear, grief, and dread that often accompany anxiety. Conditioned by a culture that pounds you with the belief that the answers are "out there," you naturally reach outward to stave off the discomfort of your inner world.

But when you find the courage to turn inward, to become curious about the labyrinths and caves that make up your inner world, everything changes. You discover that anxiety can inform your life, but it does not have to define it. You're not destined for anxiety; you're destined for equanimity. You're not destined for limitation; you're destined for greatness. You're not destined to feel lost, empty, and alone; you're destined to feel purposeful and connected. You're not destined to define yourself by your challenges; you're destined to grow through these challenges and become a more balanced version of yourself, where your weaknesses become your strengths, and the places where you've struggled most become your greatest gifts.

A library as big as the universe lives inside you, waiting for you to sit down in some dimly lit, quiet corner so that you can discover its contents. Are you ready to step inside, to unlearn much of what you've absorbed, and learn some basic principles of life and relationships that will fundamentally alter your understanding of yourself and the world? Are you ready to travel through the passageways of your four realms of self—body, mind, heart, and soul—to heed the messages that live inside each one? If so, take my hand, and let's begin.

PART ONE

ANXIETY AND ITS MESSAGES

What the frightened individual wishes above all is the
restoration of the sense of self which once worked.
What the therapist knows is that the symptoms
are helpful clues to the place of injury or neglect,
pointing the way to subsequent healing. . . . As Jung
asserted, "The outbreak of the neurosis is not just
a matter of chance. As a rule, it is most critical. It
is usually the moment when a new psychological
adjustment, a new adaptation is demanded." This
implies that our own psyche has organized this
crisis, produced this suffering, precisely because
injury has been done and change must occur.

JAMES HOLLIS
The Middle Passage: From Misery to Meaning in Midlife

1

ANXIETY DEFINED AND
THE CALL TO TURN INWARD

> Jung observed that the Aboriginal people of Australia
> spend *two-thirds* of their waking lives in some form of
> inner work. . . . We modern people can scarcely get a few
> hours free in an entire week to devote to the inner world.
>
> **ROBERT JOHNSON**
> *Inner Work: Using Dreams and Active Imagination for Personal Growth*

A sixty-year-old man bolts awake every morning at 3:00 a.m., worrying about his financial future (even though he's financially secure). A seven-year-old girl worries that her parents will die. A twenty-five-year-old woman ruminates that she doesn't love her boyfriend enough (even though he's everything she's ever wanted in a partner). These are all people who are suffering from anxiety.

While most people know what anxiety feels like, they often have a hard time describing what it is. Being able to define anxiety is one of the ways that we help to contain and soothe it, for what we can name and identify holds less charge than a nameless experience. Here's my definition of anxiety:

Anxiety is a feeling of dread, agitation, or foreboding
associated with a danger that does not exist in the
present moment. It can also be defined as a general
and pervasive sense of dis-ease without an identified

source. Anxiety, while often experienced in the body, is a head state that keeps its prisoners trapped in the realm of unproductive and fear-based thinking. Anxiety keeps you on high alert, and at its core, lives the belief that you're not okay, that you'll never be okay, and that you're not safe physically, emotionally, and/or spiritually. Anxiety and trust are mutually exclusive.

Anxiety is the catchall diagnosis du jour. Nearly everyone I know who has been sifted and sorted through the mainstream medical and psychological systems has been diagnosed with a generalized anxiety disorder. And it's not that mainstream doctors and therapists are wrong: most people are, indeed, suffering from anxiety, and the official criteria that qualify someone as having an anxiety disorder as outlined in the *Diagnostic and Statistical Manual of Mental Disorders* (known in psychological circles as the *DSM*) is very close to the definition I shared. While I agree with most components of the psychologically accepted definition of anxiety, where I diverge is in how I understand and work with it. As I've stated, I don't see it as a "disorder" at all, for when we refer to anxiety as a disorder, we label ourselves with the stamp of "Problem" and fail to recognize the profound opportunity for awakening that approaching anxiety from a mindset of respect invites. When we see anxiety as evidence of something "wrong" we miss the wisdom, the metaphors, and the opportunities for growth encased in its symptoms.

Understanding anxiety's positive function throughout history can facilitate the essential shift in mindset from wanting to get rid of it to becoming curious about it. Anxiety has always been a messenger, but the messages have altered throughout time and change from person to person. For example, being on high alert while walking in the forest when there was the possibility of encountering a tiger around the next bend once served humans extremely well. It was the sensitive people in the community who would have been attuned to the subtleties and nuances that indicated real and present danger: the slight movement of the grass, a change in temperature, an almost imperceptible sound.

Listening to and respecting anxiety's communications was a matter of life and death.

The problem now is that, without the actual tiger around the next bend, modern humans attach their anxiety onto almost any source, and then call it *intuition*. It's as if the part of the psyche that evolved to be hypervigilant to danger—the fight-or-flight response—doesn't know what to do with itself. As its primary job has been taken away, it now swerves into the path of least resistance, and this often looks like scanning the *inner* horizon for danger: Am I with the right partner? (Is love safe?) Will I harm someone? (Am I safe?) Will I have enough money? (Am I secure?) Do I have a terminal illness? (Is life safe?) Is the planet going to be okay? (Are we all safe?) We then meet these questions with the same life-or-death mindset that kept us alive in the jungle or outback, and it feels like alarm and panic. But we're in a new era, and the primal alarm system that once served us very well needs to be modernized and rechanneled so that we don't project anxiety onto others, ourselves, and the world. With millions of people suffering from anxiety worldwide, we're being called globally to recognize that embedded inside it is a powerful invitation to evolve in a new direction as a species.

Symptoms of Anxiety

Anxiety manifests in a multitude of ways, but it most commonly shows up as intrusive/incessant thoughts, symptoms in the body, and compulsive behaviors.

For my clients struggling with relationship anxiety, for example, the initial outreach email is almost always the same: "I'm in a loving, healthy relationship, but all of sudden one night I jolted awake with my heart pounding, I felt like I couldn't breathe, my mouth was dry, and I had the thought, 'I'm with the wrong partner.' Ever since then I've been plagued by incessant doubt. And when I've Googled phrases like 'How do you know when you're in love?' it only reinforces my anxiety. That must mean the thought is true." (More on real love in chapter 15.)

My clients struggling with pregnancy anxiety share: "I wanted to be pregnant more than anything, but the moment I saw the positive test result, I panicked. Now the thoughts racing through my mind day and night are so horrible. Thoughts like: I feel like I've been diagnosed with a terminal illness. I don't want this. I love my life; I'm not ready to give it up. I feel like there's an alien growing inside me. This must mean I really don't want this baby."

We'll delve more deeply into these scenarios in chapter 9 (The Realm of Thoughts), but you can see that these are the *symptoms* of anxiety—the thoughts, physical sensations, and behaviors (Googling in response to anxiety is a compulsive behavior)—and then there's the *interpretation*: "This must mean that I don't want to be in this relationship" or "This must mean I don't want this baby." When working with anxiety, it's essential to differentiate between the symptoms and the meaning we assign to those symptoms. Therefore, the more clearly you understand the symptoms of anxiety, the more readily you'll be able to name it, then approach it through the lens of curiosity and compassion without jumping to the top-layer interpretation.

Again, as much as the word *anxiety* is commonplace in today's world, many people don't know what the thoughts, feelings, and sensations are that indicate anxiety. Whatever we don't understand leads to more anxiety. If someone had told me that night I ended up in the ER after my first panic attack that I was suffering from anxiety, it would have saved me months of agony on top of the initial agony of trying to figure out what was wrong with me. Of course, there was nothing wrong with me; my soul had just brilliantly sent me the message through the messenger of panic that it was time to begin the process of individuating and breaking through the layers of my conditioned self. I wouldn't have expected the ER doctor to say, "Welcome, you've just entered your dark night of the soul." But if he had sent me on my way with information about *what* was happening, it would have been easier for me to arrive at the *why*.

Following are the most common mental, physical, and behavioral manifestations of anxiety.

INTRUSIVE THOUGHTS
- What if I'm with the wrong partner?
- What if I've missed my calling?
- What if I hurt someone?
- What if I hurt a child?
- What if the world ends?
- What if I have a terminal illness?

For an extensive list of intrusive thoughts, see p. 122.

SOMATIC SYMPTOMS
- tightness in chest
- constricted throat
- shallow breath
- antsy feeling in body—like you can't sit still
- insomnia
- dry mouth
- headaches—including pressure in the head
- muscle aches
- general feeling of dis-ease
- rapid heartbeat
- sweating
- pit in stomach
- digestion issues
- lightheadedness

BEHAVIORAL SYMPTOMS
- anger
- irritation
- addictions
- perfectionism
- incessant talking
- compulsive rituals, including online activity,
  in an attempt to seek reassurance

This is by no means an exhaustive list (it is quite extraordinary how many symptoms are manifestations of anxiety), but these are the most common ways that anxiety manifests in my worldwide cross section of clients and course members.

Origins of Anxiety

The roots of anxiety can be traced to a multitude of places—from family history, to the influence of school and religious culture, to global/cultural/societal messages. When you understand some of the origins of your anxiety, it helps to normalize it, which then softens the shame-based belief that having anxiety means that there's something wrong with you.

We know now that anxiety has a genetic component and that if one or both of your parents struggled with anxiety, you're more likely to experience anxiety as well. Not only does the predisposition toward anxiety live in your genetic makeup, but what we see role-modeled in our early life at home is also more powerful than what we're explicitly taught. In other words, if you witnessed one or both caregivers struggling with anxiety or chronic worry without seeing them take measures toward learning how to attend to it effectively, you likely absorbed that pattern. When I ask clients if either of their parents were anxious the answer is always yes.

It's important to state that even if you come from a long line of chronic worriers and one or both of your parents struggles with anxiety or depression, you're not destined to live with anxiety for the rest of your life. While this information can help you understand where you come from, it doesn't have to determine where you're going. One of the tentacles of the anxious mind is the belief that you'll *always* struggle with anxiety, that you'll *never* feel good and clear. The anxious mind tends to think in black-and-white, all-or-nothing terms, which means when you're using words like *never* and *always*, you know you're caught in anxiety's spell. As you're reading through this book, I encourage you to notice how the doom-and-gloom voice appears and try to meet it with another part of your brain that can say something like, "My past doesn't define my future. When I start to shine the light of accurate information and gentle awareness on these painful patterns, I can set myself on a new trajectory."

On one level, anxiety is sensitivity gone awry. This means that if your sensitive nature (and, again, everyone is sensitive at the core) wasn't met with gentleness and kindness, and your parents didn't know how to guide you through the big feelings of life (sadness, anger, jealousy, loneliness, disappointment, frustration, to name a few) and offer rituals or practices to help you navigate through the awareness of death but instead shamed you with messages like, "Get over it" or dismissed your big feelings because they had no idea how to tend to them (having never learned how to tend to these feelings inside themselves), the sensitivity had no choice but to morph into anxiety. In this sense, anxiety is a defense mechanism to protect you from the vulnerability of experiencing the raw feelings of being human. Anxiety, as a mental state, causes you to travel out of your heart and into the safe chambers of the mind. It was a brilliant defense mechanism that once served you well.

When I work with adult clients struggling with anxiety, I'll often ask, "Did you struggle with anxiety or worry as a child?" The answer is almost invariably yes. Interestingly, the trajectory of the manifestations of anxiety and intrusive thoughts often follows the same path: It starts as worry about something happening to their parents ("What if my mom dies?"), then shifts into intrusive thoughts about sexuality ("What if I'm gay/straight?"). To clarify here: someone who orients primarily toward heterosexuality will perseverate on the gay spike, and someone who is gay will attach onto the straight spike. It's also essential to understand that obsessive thoughts about sexual orientation have nothing to do with sexuality but are the mind's attempt to find certainty when anxiety has taken over. Seeking reassurance to try to answer this question will only reinforce the anxiety; it must be addressed at the root. From the sexuality spike the anxiety will then morph into health anxiety. And finally, when clients reach my virtual doorstep, they're in the throes of relationship or pregnancy anxiety or career anxiety. The story lines shift, but the underlying need is the same—to find certainty and safety—and it begins with the child feeling adrift on the sea of an ever-changing and overwhelming emotional life without the solid guidance of adult caregivers to hold them through the feelings until the child is able to do it themselves.

Alongside family history, there are many facets to the school system that engender anxiety, like the social pressure to conform and the academic pressure for high achievement. Furthermore, at least 20 percent of children have a learning style that is at odds with the expectations of school—children who need to move while they're learning instead of being forced to sit still, kids who are visual-spatial thinkers instead of the auditory-sequential style that schools favor, kids who are introverts and need to learn in a quiet environment instead of in a loud and crowded classroom. After many years or even days of being in a system that is out of alignment with their rhythm and temperament, children adopt the belief that there's something wrong with them, that they're broken in some way, or that they're not smart. All of which lead to anxiety.

Religion, while often offering a sense of trust in something bigger than ourselves, can also transmit the message of basic wrongness, especially around thoughts, bodies, and sexuality. When children are raised with a belief system that tells them, "If you think certain thoughts (primarily around sexuality) you have sinned," it's a setup for anxiety. Religion can also truncate one's basic sense of self-trust in that it often encourages people to place their trust exclusively in a source outside of themselves. Clients who were raised religiously and are now struggling with making a major life decision, like choosing a life partner, will often say, "What if it's not in God's plan?" This fear stems directly from the belief that there's a right and wrong way of living, and that if you don't get it right, you're destined to a life of misery and shame. This is a highly anxiety-provoking mindset.

Lastly, the media culture at large transmits anxiety in spades. Everywhere we look, we receive the message, "You're not okay. You're doing it wrong. The world is not okay. You're not safe." Now more than ever we're exposed to mindsets and images of fear, negativity, scarcity, and catastrophe on a twenty-four-hour cycle. Every time you turn on the news, you're inundated with images of disaster. Every time you look at your screen, you read about that latest political, social, or environmental downturn. Every time you see an advertisement or scroll through social media, the part of you that feels like you're not enough is activated. If part of the definition of anxiety includes the sense or belief that you're not safe, our culture has exploited this primal need to feel safe to the hilt and has created a system where we're addictively plugged in. Fear is addictive. Negativity hooks. Preying on insecurity sells. It's a vicious cycle: the more anxious we are, the more we plug in to screens, news, and technology; and the more we plug in, the more anxious we feel.

Mainstream culture, through the vessel of our screens, keeps us chronically off-kilter with the pervasive sense that we're doing it wrong. One night my son was telling me that he overheard a friend lie about her age at a birthday party, saying that she was older than she was. He asked me why she would do this, and I said, "When you're younger, the world is pressuring you to be older; and when you're older, the world tells you to look and act younger. The message is that you're never okay the way you are."

How could anyone feel anything other than anxious when these are the messages being poured daily and even hourly into our psychological water?

PRACTICE   A MEDIA DIET

To this end, one of the most effective and immediate actions you can take to temper anxiety is to go on a media diet. This means making a commitment to eliminate all social media and the news from your daily mental diet for the next thirty or more days. If that seems impossible, do it anyway. While couched in a facade of facilitating connection, social media is almost entirely focused on externals, and it's nearly impossible to go on Facebook or the news without viewing multiple horrors throughout the world and comparing ourselves to others in some way. If Facebook is a way that you communicate with friends, pick up the phone instead. And instead of texting, try calling your loved ones, or having conversations in person when possible. Texting isn't talking, and although it gives you the temporary fix of connection, it doesn't serve the bigger goal of filling yourself with healthy, meaningful connections and actions, both internal and external.

Anxiety Is Not a Game of Whac-A-Mole

When anxiety is pervasive, it takes over all your systems: body, mind, heart, and soul. In acute states of anxiety, adrenaline floods the body, which then creates the feeling that you're always on high alert, ready to fight or run from danger. In nonacute, pervasive states, anxiety manifests through chronic issues like muscle pain, headaches, difficulty getting a full breath, and insomnia. In the mental realm, my clients who struggle with intrusive thoughts describe it as a twenty-four-hour hamster wheel where they're constantly stuck on a specific thought, endlessly attempting to find an answer to create certainty. Because it is fundamentally a mental state, generalized, chronic anxiety causes people to shut down to their emotional lives, which then causes a state of numbness or emptiness. And on the level of soul, when we don't heed anxiety's attempts to reach us consciously, our dreams and nightmares, speaking in the language of metaphor and symbol, become the messengers of psyche.

Again, the mainstream model seeks to address anxiety at the level of symptom, which means trying to get rid of the symptom. But even if you can eradicate the symptom, anxiety will find another way to grab your attention. Remember: anxiety is the soul's way of communicating that something inside is awry, out of balance, or needs attention. When you ignore or remove the symptom, you miss the message, and your inner self will redouble its efforts to alert you to the need to turn inward by sending out more alarming and attention-grabbing thoughts, feelings, or physical symptoms. This is anxiety's game of Whac-A-Mole: if you whack down one mole (symptom) without addressing it from the root, another mole (symptom) will quickly appear in its place. Eventually the physical symptoms, addictions, or mental torture will reach a breaking point, and you'll have no choice but to heed the call to turn inward. At this point you'll be asked to find the courage to shift your mindset and, instead of resisting and resenting the anxiety, you can choose to approach it with curiosity, compassion, stillness, and even gratitude.

Four Key Elements: Curiosity, Compassion, Stillness, and Gratitude

There are four key elements that will help you on your path of healing from anxiety. I'm using the word *key* here intentionally, since the heroine or hero who embarks on a journey of the Self always does so with internal allies and amulets that offer help and guidance along the way. In myths and fairy tales, these helpers appear as animals, mythical creatures, or magical items that are symbols for the inner resources of strength and health that every human possesses. If anxiety is the call that leads you into the dark forest, the following inner keys are the allies and amulets that light the way.

The first key to unpacking anxiety is to make a conscious shift from protecting against, pushing away, and hating your pain to *becoming curious* about your inner world. This is not a onetime shift, but a daily, if not hourly, reset and reminder of setting the compass of your intention to the dial of curiosity. In order to do this it's essential to understand that the initial thought—be it "What if I don't love my partner?" or "What if I hurt my baby?" or "What if I have a terminal illness?"—is the distress flare; it's your inner self sounding the alarm bell. It's all the parts of you that you swept into the basement of your psyche—the messy, dark parts that struggle with uncertainty and lack of control—clamoring for your attention. It's become overcrowded down there, and it's time they come out. If you take the thoughts at face value instead of becoming curious about the deeper messages, you will miss the opportunity for healing. But when you recognize the thought as an alarm bell, you can become curious about the places inside that need your attention.

For example, a coaching client scheduled a session to talk about her conflict around moving back to her home country with her husband and six-month-old baby or staying in the United States. The obsessive thought, which sounded like, "We should move back, otherwise my daughter will grow up to be a horrible human being," had been elevated to a place of obsession where it dominated her thoughts night and day and was causing immense amounts of anxiety and aloneness. Taken at face value, her conflict seemed reasonable enough: she wanted her daughter to be raised around her extended community—her mother, sisters, and cousins—the way she herself had been raised; instead she was raising her daughter in the isolation of a big city. But when a question becomes obsessive and fear based, as evidenced by the fear that if they didn't move home, her daughter would grow up to be a horrible person, we know we're in the realm of anxiety and that the question itself is carrying storehouses of gold that need our attention. If we try to answer the question in the way the culture recommends—making pros and cons lists, asking people for advice, obsessively thinking about it—we remain caught in our heads. We not only miss the deeper wisdom about ourselves that is waiting to be gleaned, but we also eclipse the opportunity to find true direction based on deeper knowing. As Einstein famously said, "No problem can be solved from the same level of consciousness that created it," meaning that when we try to find an "answer" about an anxiety-related question from an anxious place, we only create more anxiety.

For the first part of the session, I encouraged my client to take her focus off the presenting question. This was difficult to do since she had been perseverating on the question for months, so had developed well-worn neural pathways in her brain that reinforced the message that answering it was a matter of life and death. This is how anxiety works: it hooks into a question or theme like a dog with a bone, and you become hell-bent on answering it in the belief that if you could only answer this one question, you would find peace.

But as we spiraled in and dropped down out of the realm of thoughts, my client began to make connections. She could see that the thought had taken on mythic proportions the moment she got pregnant—as often happens in transitions—and she could see many areas embedded in the thought that needed her attention: her grief about being far from home and attending to a layer of sadness that she had moved away ten years earlier in order to preserve her sense of self; the longing to return home as a metaphor for her longing to return to her internal home as she made sense of some painful aspects of her childhood; her grief about leaving her daughter to go back to work; and more. Once she attended to these areas, she could make a decision based on clarity instead of frantic anxiety. Once the messages encased in anxiety are discovered, the initial thought dissolves and clarity is achieved.

PRACTICE BECOME CURIOUS BY NOTICING AND NAMING

Begin by taking about fifteen to twenty minutes to write down what anxiety feels like and how it manifests for you. Be curious! Remind yourself that anxiety is not your enemy but your messenger, and begin to inquire what messages it wants to deliver.

The first step toward breaking free from anxiety is to *notice* when it appears, and then *name* how it shows up for you. To encourage the mindset of curiosity, ask yourself questions like: Where do I feel anxiety in my body? What thoughts or themes are connected to my anxiety now and in the past? What is my first memory of anxiety? How was my sensitivity and then my anxiety handled by my caregivers as a young person?

Every time an anxious thought or feeling arises name it out loud by saying, "Anxiety. That's an intrusive thought." If you can, make notes throughout the day when you notice your anxiety. The notes section of your phone works well to this end, but keeping a handwritten journal is even better.

The second key element in finding healing is to learn to meet your anxiety with compassion. This means replacing the lifelong habit of responding to your difficult feelings and experiences with shame with a kinder response that allows you to be wherever you are. Given that most people received the message growing up that difficult feelings are "bad" and are to be ignored, shamed, or silenced, this isn't an easy task. We will be exploring more deeply throughout the book how to rewire the habitual shame response—and in many ways the entire paradigm of this book is predicated on shifting from a mindset of rejecting anxiety to one of accepting it—but for now, I would like to teach you one of the simplest practices for learning to meet yourself with kindness: Tonglen.

PRACTICE TONGLEN

One of the most effective practices for reversing the habit of pushing away unwanted feelings is the Buddhist practice of Tonglen, which was introduced to this country by the American Buddhist nun Pema Chödrön. This on-the-spot practice is very simple. Breathe in what we normally think of as "not wanted" and breathe out what's wanted or, as Pema Chödrön teaches on her site, "When you do Tonglen *on the spot*, simply breathe in and breathe out, taking in pain and sending out spaciousness and relief." What's so powerful about this practice is that it goes against how we habitually respond to painful feelings, so when we practice it over time, we retrain our minds to accept and even welcome pain and fear (in all their manifestations).

Next, see if you can connect to the second step of Tonglen: Breathe into the pain of everyone else on the planet who is feeling lonely, sad, disappointed, overwhelmed, and heartbroken at this very moment, and breathe out love and connection. If you think you're the only one having a hard time with life, think again. In some strange and beautiful way, we're all in this together, and when you can connect to the invisible web of heart-strands that connect us in pain and in beauty, something opens up inside and anxiety quiets down. ✑

The third key for healing from anxiety is to carve out time and space every day to slow down into stillness. We cannot decipher the messages of anxiety when we're moving at light speed, for the soul moves in organic time, not technological time. When we fill every free moment with busyness, work, distractions, perpetual motion, texting, talking, listening to music, scrolling, clicking, and watching, we lose our capacity to hear and connect with our inner selves. In fact, one of the messages that anxiety brings is an alarm bell that says, "Slow down! I can't hear myself think. I have no time for self-reflection. When I lose touch with my inner world, I don't know who I am, and I feel anxious." Our culture is moving faster by the day, and our souls can't keep up.

Every practice I teach in this book requires slowing down. You can slow down for a brief pause, where you engage in a mindful moment, like at a stoplight when you choose to breathe deeply and notice your surroundings instead of checking your phone or changing the music. You can slow down for longer periods, like at the beginning and end of each day when you take time to journal, meditate, or simply be in quiet reflection. Part of the work of breaking free from anxiety includes positive action, like committing to the practices that I teach, and some of it includes taking time to slow down into a space of nourishing silence and literally doing nothing, like sitting next to a tree or lying in the grass without your phone in sight. In the space of stillness, the keys of curiosity and compassion constellate as allies to aid you on your journey of healing.

PRACTICE MEDITATIVE QUESTIONS TO HELP YOU SLOW DOWN

From a place of curiosity, ask yourself:

- What happens when I take time to sit under the umbrella of a sacred moment? When, instead of taking a photo of the moment and posting it on Instagram, I listen fully to my solitude and silence until I can hear the raindrops of my soul watering my own soil?

- What happens if, when I wake up in the morning— when my eyelids slowly, achingly open to meet the morning light—instead of reaching for my phone to scroll and click, I reach for the dream image that is still playing on the edges of consciousness before the image evaporates like bubbles in air?

- What might happen if, at the day's end, I pause at an open window long enough to look up into the night sky and receive the wisdom of the moonlight? What secrets might she whisper down on silver threads?

What happens is that you come face-to-face with yourself in *this moment*, in present time. In those brief moments of silence and solitude, you meet your pain.

Yes, the parts of you that you've stuffed away because they were deemed unlovable in early years, but also, if you can dare to imagine, your places of light: the poem that longs to be written, the song that needs to be sung, the sweet tears of grief that are waiting to fall into your cupped hands.

The fourth key, and one that helps you shift into curiosity and develop more self-compassion, is to set the dial of your inner compass to gratitude. This means being grateful not only for the obvious blessings that abound in your life, but also for the challenges. As Brother David Steindl-Rast shares in his audio series *A Grateful Heart*: "Coming alive is becoming alert and aware to the thousands and thousands of blessings that we receive—even on a day on which we have to go to the dentist or on a day we are really sick."

This is what it means to see the gift in anxiety. It's through our challenges that we learn and grow the most, which means embedded in every anxious feeling or intrusive thought, hidden inside the nightmare of a panic attack and the grueling path of insomnia, are diamonds that, when properly mined, lead to healing and serenity. It's difficult to imagine at the outset of your journey, but every single course member and client I've worked with who has embraced this path of approaching their anxiety with the keys of curiosity, compassion, and stillness leading the way comes back to say, "I didn't believe you when you said that I would feel grateful for my anxiety, but I really do. Meeting my anxiety in this way has brought me home to myself in ways I couldn't begin to imagine when I was in the thick of it." The same can be true for you.

I encourage you to take the keys of curiosity, compassion, stillness, and gratitude with you as you read through this book and work with your anxiety. You don't know what diamonds you'll find inside your anxiety, what messages are hiding inside your intrusive thoughts, what gifts are embedded in illness. These gems will be different for everyone, as there is no one-size-fits-all formula for healing, but as you do this inner work, you'll find a level of serenity, empowerment, and clarity that you never knew possible. You'll discover that you're okay, that there's a beauty and symmetry to the world that you never quite understood, and that there's a purpose for your life. The tight places will loosen. Your breath will deepen. You'll know, perhaps for the first time in your life, who you really are.

PRACTICE BELLY BREATHING

Deep belly breathing is one of the most commonly recommended on-the-spot practices to calm your nervous system and, thus, anxiety. The reason for this is that when you breathe deeply, pushing your belly out all the way like a balloon, your vagus nerve is activated in such a way that it calms your amygdala, the emotional response center deep within your brain. Even taking five deep breaths—slow inhales that fill your belly and slow exhales that compress it—will calm your nervous system and offer a small reset that will help you move into the next moment with more ease.

Next time you notice your telltale signs of anxiety, stop for one minute, and follow these simple steps:

1. Place your hand on your lower belly, below your belly button. (Placing your hand on your body, when done intentionally, is an act of self-love.)

2. Inhale as deeply as you can, pushing your belly out like it's a balloon. (If you can't inhale very deeply, don't worry. A common anxiety symptom is difficulty taking a deep breath, so when people say "Take a deep breath," it can activate more anxiety. Just push your belly out as far as you can.)

3. Hold your breath for one second.

4. Exhale slowly.

5. Repeat four more times.

Belly breathing is one of the on-the-spot practices I mentioned in the introduction that can be done anywhere, at any time. Remember: the more you engage with these practices, the more you'll rewire your habitual response to anxiety from one of fear and contraction to one of expansion and acceptance. The more you can expand around the symptoms of anxiety, the more you'll be able to learn from them and continue to move forward on your path of healing.

2

TWO CULTURAL MESSAGES THAT CREATE ANXIETY

The Myth of Normal and the Expectation of Happiness

> As human beings, our job in life is to help people realize how rare and valuable each one of us really is, that each of us has something that no one else has—or ever will have—something inside that is unique to all time. It's our job to encourage each other to discover that uniqueness and to provide ways of developing its expression.
>
> FRED ROGERS

At the center of anxiety, intrusive thoughts, and lack of fulfillment lives a common source: lack of self-trust. Self-trust is the crystal compass at the center of being that allows us to navigate through our inner and outer worlds with ease and confidence. It helps us discern loving thoughts from faulty thoughts and attend to our emotional life with compassion. Without self-trust, it's difficult to make decisions. Whether it's a major decision like accepting a job, or a minor decision like what to order at a restaurant, people struggling with anxiety often find themselves frozen like a deer in the headlights when it comes time to decide.

The underlying fear is of making the "wrong" choice: a mistake that they'll regret, succumbing to the belief that perfection is possible, or that they're missing out. We're so deeply conditioned to believe that there's a right or wrong choice that when it comes time to make even minor decisions in life, we're scared of messing up. It's like we believe that there's a multiple-choice test for every decision, and if we fill in the wrong circle, we'll fail; or conversely, if we answer "correctly," the holy grail of eternal happiness will be revealed.

What we don't learn is that self-trust and well-being, which are the opposite of anxiety, can only be accessed when we connect to our inner wellsprings of wisdom and wholeness. This wholeness lives inside of you, buried underneath the self-doubt that arose as a result of others telling you what to do, like, feel, and think. If you observe a baby, you'll quickly see that we are born knowing what we like and don't like, when we're hungry, tired, or need connection. We know ourselves quite well at birth, and it's only as a result of well-meaning parents, teachers, doctors, other adults, and caregivers that our innate self-trust is damaged. Anxiety, when approached through the lens of wisdom, is the guide that will lead the way back to yourself. Let's examine how our self-trust was damaged before delving into how it's repaired.

The Myth of Normal

It can be argued that the idea of "normal" is at the root of self-doubt, and as such, is one of the most psychologically damaging ideas ever to hit modern culture. For lurking just behind the pervasive and negative running commentary of "What's wrong with me?" that affects most of my clients is the question, "Why can't I just be normal?"

But what *is* normal? Normal is trying to squeeze yourself into a narrow range of what our society views as acceptable behavior. It's living life on mute because your loud sounds and bright colors or sensitive ways don't fit the mold. It's cutting off the flares of who you really are because they don't fit into the watered-down definition of a "regular" person. It's not standing out, making sure you're neither too smart nor too dumb, neither too social nor too quiet, neither too confident nor too insecure, but living life in the gray places and the safe zones.

The expectation of normal was likely imprinted onto you *in utero* as the doctor compared your growth chart to other "typically" growing fetuses. The comparisons continued throughout your nine-month stay in the womb, as your mother faithfully attended her prenatal checkups and received confirmation—either via ultrasound, amniocentesis, or palpations—that you were *normal*. Perhaps the news wasn't good, and the reports showed an "abnormality," in which case waves of anxiety were sent down the telegraph of the umbilical cord with the message of, "Oh, no. Something's wrong. Baby isn't growing according to the standard." The comparisons against normal continued at birth, and then at each well-baby visit, at your annual checkups, and of course, once you started school. Well-meaning parents and teachers were in quiet, unconscious collusion to make sure that you were "normal," and any deviance was quickly nipped in the bud.

If you were a "good" girl or boy and had the social and academic skills to fit in, you probably learned the rules very early on and managed to do your own nipping. You siphoned off the "weird" stuff. You snipped at the "un-prettiness." Lest you were made fun of, you quickly tucked away somewhere deep inside you any unusual behaviors. You achieved *normal* and continued on through your life until something broke you open, likely when the manifestations of anxiety reached a breaking point, and you began to unpack the real you living in the shadow realm.

If you didn't or couldn't achieve normal, life was probably more painful in your younger years. While the other kids seemed to "get the rules," you simply couldn't sit still. How many times did your teacher say to you, with clear exasperation, "Why can't you just be *normal*?" You tried to sit still, you tried to snip off the "weird" stuff, but something in your wiring wouldn't allow you to do it. You plodded through school as best you could, and if you made it to college, you likely found a world that, at last, accepted you as you were, weirdness and all. In some ways, you were one of the lucky ones: because of your inability to conform to the system, your authentic self remained more intact. Nevertheless, the pain that the outcasts typically endure during their younger years leaves scars deep and wide.

What's fascinating to understand is that *normal* is a fairly recent notion. As Jonathan Mooney, who struggled with a variety of learning disorders in his younger years, writes in *The Short Bus: A Journey Beyond Normal*:

> As I drove, I thought about that word *normal*. Before leaving on this trip, I had come across a great book called *Enforcing Normalcy* by Lennard David, who makes a strong argument that the word *normalcy* did not enter the English language until around 1860. Before then, we had only the concept of the ideal, which no one would ever hope to obtain. In the United States, *normal* arose within a cultural context as the nation sought to control a growing urban population and Americanize immigrants from around the world. Normalcy, though, is first and foremost an idea that arises from statistics. *The normal, norm, or normalcy do not exist in the real world of real people* [emphasis mine], despite the fact that we are told that we can modify our behavior and train our bodies and minds to reach it. We are told to chase it—in our culture, in our families, in our lives. But when we chase it—as I did—it disappears. Normalcy is like a horizon that keeps receding as you approach it.

Chasing the receding horizon of normal results in massive amounts of anxiety, for the implicit message is, once again, that you're not okay as you are. The tragedy is that we spend our early years trying to cram ourselves into the "normal" box only to learn later in life that the people we revere most are those who dared to live outside the box. Then we're left with the daunting task—in our late twenties at the earliest and most often at midlife—of excavating the buried parts of ourselves and relearning what it means to be fully alive and fully ourselves. Wouldn't it have been so much easier if we had been encouraged to be ourselves from the beginning, recognizing that human beings come in all shapes, sizes, and variances, and that it's these exact variances that create the colors that render us fully alive? Wouldn't it be so much healthier to eradicate the concept of "normal" completely from childhood expectations and allow children to be who they are without apology?

PRACTICE HOW THE MYTH OF NORMAL HAS AFFECTED YOU

Take some time to reflect and write about how the expectation of normal has affected your self-concept, your life choices, and your anxiety. When do you first remember being told, either explicitly or covertly, that you were wrong in some way, and as a result, you abdicated an aspect of yourself in an attempt to conform? What do you know about your mother's pregnancy, your birth, your infancy and toddler years, and your school years that may have contributed to the belief that you were wrong or abnormal in some way? Do you remember being told "You were such a difficult baby" or "You were such a good boy"? These statements, while commonplace, reinforce the belief that there's one right way to be.

Come back to this exercise as you reflect on this concept and allow the statements and memories that contributed to the belief that there's something wrong with you rise to the surface. 🍃

The Expectation of Happiness

The second prominent cultural message that leads to anxiety is the expectation of happiness and the denial of shadow. We live in a culture that chases the light and abhors the darkness; in fact, "the pursuit of happiness" is one of the guiding principles upon which American culture is predicated. We worship the happy face and plaster on smiles when we venture into the world. Easygoing babies statistically receive more praise than fussy babies, and bubbly teens garner more positive attention than surly ones. In a culture that upholds the extrovert ideal as the pinnacle of personality types, we absorb the message early in life that if we're prone to a more melancholic temperament, there must be something wrong with us. "Keep it light," we learn. "Keep it peppy," we hear. Sweep away the messy, unraveled, chaotic, loud parts of life and of yourself. Hide them in the dark.

You're sold the message early on that attaining happiness requires following the expectations and timeline of the culture: do well in school (even if it's opposed to your learning style), have a lot of friends (even if you're an introvert and prefer one or two close friends), play sports if you're a boy (even if you prefer to read or do art), attend college when you're eighteen (even if your chosen path doesn't require a college degree), party hard (even if that's not your style), and then find a great job, get married, buy a house, have a baby, work harder and harder and harder as you climb the corporate ladder, have a second baby, make a lot of money, buy a bigger house and more expensive car, retire. In that order. Some part of you knows that following this formula doesn't guarantee happiness, but unless you consciously choose against the prescriptions of the culture, you're likely to fall into the sheep line and blindly follow along. In doing so, you abdicate the beautiful intricacies of your unique personality, your gifts, traits, needs, desires, and most especially, any aspects of yourself that fall outside the box.

If young people were taught early in life how to orient not toward happiness but instead toward meaning and fulfillment, a significant amount of their anxiety would be reduced. Instead of transmitting the message of happiness, we need to send a message of wholeness. This means that parents would receive the message from every source—pediatricians, teachers, clergy, friends, media—that there is so much more that is right with their children than wrong, and that the goal for their children is not necessarily happiness but a life of purpose, with a solid sense of self-trust leading the way.

·PRACTICE   REPLACING "SHOULD" WITH LOVING ACTION

One of the fastest ways to recognize that you're outsourcing your self-trust is to listen when the word *should* populates your thoughts and vocabulary. As soon as I hear a "should" statement, I know that a client is suffering from an externally imposed expectation and is inevitably comparing her- or himself to a cultural ideal of "good" or "right" behavior, which then creates anxiety.

For example, let's take the statement: "I should feel more excited to see my partner." We carry a cultural idea that if you're away from your partner and not pining for him or her, it's an indication that something is wrong or missing from the relationship. Our minds then go to: *I'm not in love enough* or *I'm with the wrong person*, and the anxious spiral begins.

To heal from the "should" mindset, start to notice how often the word enters your self-talk, and then notice how you feel inside when you fall prey to believing the "should" statement. When you hear the word *should*, instead ask, "What would be most loving to myself and others right now?"

There Are No Answers, Only Guideposts to Wisdom

There have been times when I have wanted to collapse from the overpowering wave of not knowing that washed over me in moments of conflict or overwhelm: my boys at each other's throats, my husband and I in an argument, a temporary falling out with a soul-sister, the state of the world or the homeless man on the corner. The pain seemed to storm around me like the fluttering of a thousand moths, a hurricane of emotions tipping into a flicker of despair from the awareness that we all struggle and nobody has the answers. Where's the magic wand? Where's the ultimate in-the-trenches parenting manual that teaches us how to ensure our kids will get along and be okay? How do we solve the world's pain? Does anyone have the answers?

But then something else takes over. It usually arrives in the aftermath of repair when someone has come forward with the courageous act of true accountability and the other person receives it. These moments of vulnerability soften me into submission, an acceptance that while we don't know what we're doing, maybe we don't have to know. It reminds me of the famous lines from one of Rilke's letters:

> Be patient toward all that is unsolved in your heart and try
> to love the questions themselves, like locked rooms and
> like books that are now written in a very foreign tongue.
> Do not now seek the answers, which cannot be given you
> because you would not be able to live them. And the point
> is, to live everything. Live the questions now. Perhaps you
> will then gradually, without noticing it, live along some
> distant day into the answer.

Part of what trips us up is that we expect life and relationships to be easy. There is nothing easy about life, and relationships especially seem to stir up every hidden demon, every dusty complex, every latent unshed tear from our own life and our parents' histories hidden away in the attics of their psyches. Relationships ask us to grow in ways that nothing else does or can. And yet, for example, when we don't feel like kissing our partner we wonder what's wrong. When our kids are struggling, we wonder what's wrong. When we don't hear back from a friend, we wonder what's wrong. We search for answers and usually end up feeling worse about ourselves, falling prey to the implicit message that says, "If you follow my advice, your kid or relationship or life will be conflict-free and effortless."

A more comforting and realistic mindset is to know that every moment of flow is a small miracle: when my open heart aligns with your open heart and we experience closeness together; when the kids find their way to a creative game that satisfies them both; when friendship flows for weeks or months or years on end without a blip—all this is evidence of love at work. Why? Because there are so many ways that our hearts close, when fear or jealousy or negative habits prevail and prevent others from merging with your river, that when two open hearts meet in a cosmic, joyous collision—when your desire to kiss aligns with my desire to be kissed—it's a moment of grace.

We are all unformed: you, me, our partners, friends, and kids. Even people we hold up as figures of completion or perfection—the Dalai Lama, Mother Teresa, Jesus, Pema Chödrön—are and were raw as well. The difference is that, as a result of years of dedicated practice, they're able to move toward their raw spots with love and compassion. They probably react less impulsively than most people, and when they do "act out," they move toward the reaction with curiosity. We all have this capacity. It just takes practice and rewiring to cultivate it.

It's deeply comforting to know that we're not alone in our imperfections. The path of comparisons, which is deeply rooted in the myth of normal and the expectation of happiness, is unhelpful at best and dangerous at worst. The path to liberation lies in cultivating a more loving and realistic relationship with life, one that recognizes that there is no finish line, that we are all unformed. Instead of attempting to squeeze ourselves into the unattainable expectations that the culture espouses, we learn to access more self-love as we journey on this painful, glorious planet together.

To Be Human

If you're not meant to pretzel yourself into the myth of normal and the expectation of happiness, what are you meant to do? Instead of striving for happiness and normal, let's strive to be human, which isn't striving at all but a gentle allowing of ourselves to be exactly as we are. What does it mean to be human? When you're struggling to free yourself from the negative and limiting expectations and messages of the culture, I invite you to read the following statements as reminders.

> To be human is to remember that this being human is
> an experiment without a goal or destination, but with
> a plan that includes learning about love at its center.

> To be human is to love awkwardly and without skill, for
> how can we practice that which we never learned or saw?
> We will sit with our partner in a cesspool of pain and silent
> confusion and have no idea how to climb out. We will feel
> connected and alive, and then disconnected and alone. We
> will doubt and exhale, find peace and forget again. This is
> what it is to love another with hearts that have been hurt
> and souls that have not yet learned how to love fully.

> To be human is to feel uncomfortable even with
> the people we love most in the world.

> To be human is to forget to connect to gratitude, to
> forget to take care of ourselves, to forget to pray. Perhaps
> we spend more time forgetting than remembering,
> which makes those brief dips in the sparkling pool
> of remembering ever more delicious and divine.

> To be human is to grow toward an acceptance of paradox
> and widen our capacity to tolerate uncertainty until
> we say "I don't know" more often than "I know."

> To be human is to struggle. Eventually we realize that when
> we sit under the umbrella of "shoulds"—"This shouldn't be so
> hard. I should be happy."—the pain rains down harder. But
> when we accept the fact that anxiety, depression, loneliness,
> powerlessness, grief, joy, and exhilaration are all part of the
> design, we step out into the rain and perhaps even dance a little.

To be human is to grieve even when we don't know
why we're grieving, to feel afraid even when we
don't know why we're scared, and to feel joyful even
when we don't know the source of our joy.

To be human is to make mistakes, and sometimes this means
that we will hurt others, whether our closest loved ones or
people we've never met. To be human is to say, "I'm sorry. I
hope you can forgive me" as we dance a dance of closeness
and pain, remorse and forgiveness, rupture and repair.

To be human is to experience times of ease and flow alternating
with times of struggle. When we identify too closely with the
struggle, we fall into despair. When we attach too deeply into
ease, we slip into hubris. Just as a raft navigates the still waters
and the rapids, so we float and fight along this river of life.

To be human is to long to be seen with the perfect attunement
of a new mother, and yet to know that there is no such thing
as perfect attunement. In moments of clarity and wisdom,
we remember that the only perfect seeing comes from our
relationship to source, the divine, the one breath. In those
loving and invisible arms, we are seen, known, and loved.

To be human is to have hidden caverns inside the
labyrinth of psyche, shadowlands that you cannot see
or know until you're cracked open. From the fissure,
the light floods in and illuminates the shadow, causing
what lives below to fly up into consciousness.

To be human is to realize that your partner and your friends
also have these shadow regions, places of darkness that you
cannot see or know, in the beginning or even for years. Then
one day, he or she is cracked open, and the furies fly to the
surface, asking to be known, asking to be loved into healing.

To be human is to have blind spots. No matter how much we delve into the interior realms, there will always be places we cannot see ourselves. This is why the most honest and courageous question we can ask a trusted loved one is, "What am I not seeing?" And when the blind spots are illuminated, we sing a song of gratitude that another veil of illusion and mis-seeing has been lifted.

To be human is to age. The fine lines in your thirties will deepen to creases in your forties and fifties and beyond. Because we live in a culture that tries to erase the lines, we're forgetting that our lines tell the stories of our lives: "Look, that's when I laughed so hard, I cried. Look, that's when I cried so hard, I crumpled into silence." And where are the silver-haired women? They're being dyed out of the culture, so fierce is our fight against time. What we don't often see is that with aging comes wisdom, with time comes acceptance, and with the shortening of days comes the lengthening of gratitude.

To be human is to serve, whether it's the patch of earth outside your dwelling, the furry creature at your feet, the people with whom you share a home, or in a broader, more public context. One form of serving isn't superior to any other. When the service overflows from the waters of the well of self, we connect to the source and to a place of meaning. As Jane Goodall says, "You cannot get through a single day without having an impact on the world around you. What you do makes a difference, and you have to decide what kind of difference you want to make."

To be human is to connect to every other being on the planet, not just through information but through the brain of the heart that opens with strength and courage until the young, limp boy being carried from the water in the arms of an aching soldier is my son, and his mother is my sister, and from across all the seas and lands of this vast yet small planet she collapses in my arms, and I hold her there, the grief of my prayers catching her in an invisible blanket.

To be human is to love and be loved as best we can, and to remove the barriers that prevent us from loving fully and freely so that we can bring our love into the world that so desperately needs us.

To be human is to know that we are imperfect and whole: we will hurt and be hurt; we will feel disappointed and will disappoint; we will stumble and fall and get back up again.

PRACTICE NOTICING YOUR INTRINSIC, POSITIVE TRAITS

Let's pause here to take some time to begin the process of rewiring what's "wrong" and focus on what's right, whole, and healthy. The most effective way to do this is to write an appreciation list of who you are in your highest, most essential self. This isn't a list of your achievements, degrees, or anything external. Rather, it's a list of your intrinsic, inviolable qualities that speak to your character and your heart. For example, when I ask course members to do this exercise, they will often share things like: "I'm a kind and giving person. I care about animals. I like the way my nose crinkles when I smile, and I have a good sense of humor. I know my sensitivity is a gift, even if I don't always see it that way. It helps me in my work, and it helps me to be a good friend. I work on myself, and I try to learn and grow. I'm here, taking this course (or reading this book), which is one way that I'm trying to grow."

I suggest including this exercise in your morning or evening journaling. It is a way to rewire the habit of seeing the glass as half-empty (focusing on what's wrong) to a new habit of seeing the glass as half full (focusing on your goodness and wholeness) and embracing the mindset that you're okay exactly as you are.

3

ROADBLOCKS TO HEALING

> Anxiety is not optional in life. It's part of life. We
> come into life through anxiety. And we look at it and
> remember it and say to ourselves: We made it. We
> got through it. In fact, the worst anxieties and the
> worst tight spots in our life, often, years later, when
> you look back at them, reveal themselves as the
> beginning of something completely new. . . . And
> that can give us courage . . . in looking forward and
> saying: Yes, this is a tight spot. It's about as tight a spot
> as the world has ever been in, or at least humankind.
> But, if we go with it . . . it will be a new birth. And
> that is trust in life. And this going with it means
> you look [and ask], what is the opportunity[?]
>
> BROTHER DAVID STEINDL-RAST

The Character of Resistance

Even if we can touch down into our intrinsic wholeness and shine
the light of curiosity on our wounds from a place of compassion, we
can still experience roadblocks on the journey of healing. Many of
you, I'm sure, have had the experience of starting a new practice—like
meditating or making green smoothies every morning, both of which
can help with anxiety—only to find that within a week or a month,
you've fallen off the horse. Why is that?

It's because of the inner character of resistance, which I talked
about in the introduction. Why would we resist growth and healing

when they can only lead to positive change? The answer is in the question: it's the *change* itself that is terrifying. We all have a part of us that longs to remain in the realm of the familiar, safe, and predictable, and it's this part that resists our attempts to grow.

Resistance, which is a cousin of fear, manifests as feeling too lazy, scared, or tired to engage in the practices or actions that you know will serve your higher self. It's the part that would rather binge on Netflix at the end of the day instead of write in your journal. It's the part that would rather sit on the couch than go for a run. The more you can name when resistance is running the show, the easier it will be to choose against it in service of your intention to heal and grow. To help with the naming, here are some of the key characteristics of resistance/fear:

- It clings to the status quo.

- It needs control at all costs.

- It's terrified of change in any form, especially inner change.

- It's solid in form, not soft or shifting.

- It feels safest when life moves along without any change in rhythm or habits.

- It abhors risk.

- It's terrified of trusting.

- It has a misguided illusion of control and believes that if it worries enough it can prevent bad things from happening.

- It's impatient and wants things to be resolved right now.

- It can't tolerate paradox and thinks in black-and-white terms.

- It feels safer in your head, meaning it doesn't like to spend time in the realm of feelings. It associates feelings with being out of control, since that's how they felt as a child, and the worst thing for this part of you is to feel out of control.

- It thrives on laziness and loves to stagnate you in inertia.

There are other reasons why we resist growth. Growing means taking responsibility for ourselves in all ways. The child part of us that longs for someone else to rescue us from our pain becomes very loud when we consider taking on this task ourselves. I've worked with many clients who, as adults, are still operating from the belief, often unconsciously, that it's someone else's job to take care of them, especially their parents, and that if they assume that responsibility, then their parents never will. Of course, their parents never will anyway, but the resistant part of them doesn't want to acknowledge that.

Here's another aspect of resistance and self: Jungian psychology teaches us that resistance itself is part of the plan. It's not just something to get over or hate, but our resistance, because it provides something to push up against, helps us grow. It's not any more helpful to think of resistance as a bad part of our personality than it is to think of anxiety as the enemy. Rather, like anxiety, resistance is an essential aspect of self that, when attended to and worked with effectively, aids our healing process. In other words, by working with resistance, we strengthen our sense of self. It's all exactly as it's meant to be; none of it is an accident.

You can see this principle at play in our political sphere. Regardless of your beliefs, you can see that the greatest amount of change occurs when there's a force to push against. We seem to need something to push against in order to initiate growth, both in the outer sphere and in the inner one. This helps us view all parts of ourselves—including our resistance—as inner friends that are here to help us heal and move toward wholeness.

Is it possible to break through resistance? Absolutely. A colleague and I once had an invigorating conversation about how one of the most challenging and rewarding aspects of our work is helping clients break through the wall of resistance that prevents them from taking full responsibility for their well-being. On the surface, it looks like all these clients want to feel better—otherwise why would they be seeking help?—but resistance works undercover and often emerges through the back door. While they want to feel better, they don't always want to do the inner work that will allow them to feel better. It's even deeper than that: they may *want* to want to do the work, but when their resistance is ironclad, it wields all of the power. They are powerless. Until they're not; until they're able to do enough of the work that they can break through the roadblock and shift from stuckness to movement.

Many people are so identified with their shame-and-pain stories that they're scared to shift out of that identity; they would rather remain miserable than take the risk of stepping into a new story. Remember: resistance clings to the familiar at all costs, even if what's familiar is making you miserable. If you're battling with resistance, ask yourself this cut-through question: Am I ready to make my own healing more important than this current identity? If so, then sit still and listen for the answer.

Following are clues that you're avoiding responsibility and are stuck behind a wall of resistance:

- Your focus is almost exclusively on the key to happiness as something external. This can take the form of being single and tortured by the question of whether or not you made the right decision to leave your partner, or being with a partner and ruminating on one aspect of the relationship that isn't fulfilling you.

- You're obsessed with a single question that occupies a significant amount of your time and energy. This is usually an intrusive thought, but can appear as an obsessive question like "Should I change jobs?" or "Did I make a mistake?"

- You feel stuck on your healing path. You've tried many different modalities, programs, courses, books, and so on, and none of them "work." This is usually an indicator that resistance is preventing you from actually doing the work and is instead hoping for a magic fix.

- When you're honest with yourself, you realize that you want someone else to fix and rescue you (your mother, father, partner, friend, or therapist).

I have worked with many clients who, regardless of the specifics of the resistance story or the underlying reasons why it wields power, were able to break through it and begin the work of reclaiming their life. If you commit to your inner work and call on the resource of patience—while continually naming resistance every time it tries to sabotage your attempts to heal—*and* choose the counteraction, you will break through as well.

PRACTICE WORKING WITH RESISTANCE

Take some time to write down how resistance shows up for you. The more familiar you become with this internal character, the easier it will be to identify it when it shows up. When you notice that resistance is in the driver's seat, try the following three actions to help you break through:

1. **Name it.** We can't change what we're not aware of, and for many people, simply realizing that they're in resistance helps them to shift out of it.

2. **Ask for help from a greater source.** Even if you can't seem to stay with the inner work but want to, you can ask for help: "Please help me commit to my own growth. Please help me take responsibility." By the way, religion doesn't own the copyright on prayer. If you have posttraumatic God syndrome, pray to your own higher self. Pray to the Universe. Pray to the ocean, to life force, to healing. You don't even have to believe in the power of prayer. Do it anyway.

3. **Harness your inner loving father.** The loving father is the masculine energy inside of you that says, "I know you don't want to do it, but we're doing it anyway." The healthy inner father is decisive, clear thinking, firm with love, and doesn't indulge in resistant voices that say, "I don't feel like it." It's the parent who says to the child, "I know you don't want to go to [piano, martial arts, acting] class, but every time you go, you're happy you went, so we're going anyway." This is *not* the part that forces someone to do something that is truly not in their best interest, but rather the part that is connected to the highest good and pushes through the resistance in service of that aim. It's the part that knows that that fundamental laziness is part of being human and that resistance, which never wants to change, clings to what is easy and familiar. Remember: resistance loves sitting in front of the television for a Netflix bingefest instead of getting up and going for a brisk walk. If you want to break free from anxiety, you must act against fundamental laziness until the new, loving habit takes hold.

Working with resistance is one of the hardest elements of healing. And while it's important to recognize that sometimes there's wisdom in resistance, it's equally important to keep working with it, patiently and with commitment, until a window of light opens inside. Because the bottom-line, tough-love truth is that nobody is going to save you: not your relationship, not a different job or house or city, not your parents, not your therapist. There's no escape hatch for life. We must bring awareness to all the tricky ways that resistance takes hold—the thoughts, the propensity toward inertia, allowing ourselves to become swallowed up in intrusive pain—and then access and grow our stronger inner parts that are working in service of our wholeness and healing.

Responsibility: The Key to Transformation

Taking responsibility for our well-being is an essential key to transformation. We cannot heal if we're waiting for someone else to heal us and if we're committed to a mindset of blame and refusal. Along with resistance, one of the ways that people refuse responsibility is by subscribing to the belief that their suffering shouldn't be happening: that if something external were different, they wouldn't be struggling with anxiety. As discussed, we're so culturally addicted to the belief that our internal states are determined by external circumstances that it's like swimming upstream to develop a different mindset—one that invites taking 100 percent responsibility for our pain. The belief that anxiety shouldn't be happening stops people dead in their tracks from doing the work that needs to be done. This is fighting against reality, because the anxiety *is* happening, and every time you fall prey to the escape-hatch mindset you miss the opportunity you're being given to heal and grow.

Growing a Loving Inner Parent

An essential component to taking responsibility is accessing the loving parent at the helm of our ship. Paradoxically, a significant aspect of this work is about growing this loving parent. How do we access something we don't have? We recognize that the belief of "I don't have a loving parent" isn't actually true. It's one of resistance's tactics to tell you that you don't have an inner adult, and therefore, you can't take responsibility for yourself.

We all have this part of us. Every time you offer support to a friend in need, you're accessing your own inner compassionate friend. Every time you hold loving space for your son or daughter to feel their feelings, you're accessing the inner parent. Every time you connect to your wisdom, that place below thoughts and feelings, you're touching into your wise self. Every time you take care of your body, heart, mind, or soul in a loving and attentive way, you're acting from your loving adult. Every time you take care of your pet, you're being a loving caregiver.

The definition of a wise self/inner parent is:

> The solid, compassionate, curious part of you that takes loving care of you in all four realms—physical, emotional, mental, and spiritual. It is the part of you that can access wisdom to counteract faulty beliefs, can hold emotional pain without being swallowed by it, and works with resistance in effective ways so that you can continue to carve out time daily for your practices and inner work.

When someone is first starting to try to change their negative self-talk, they realize that they would never say to a friend the things they say to themselves. This is a very good starting point. Next time you're feeling sad or anxious, imagine how you might respond to a friend or a child who was feeling that way. The dialogue might look like this (to learn the dialogue journaling method, see appendix B):

> **Fear.** I'm feeling scared. I'm scared I might have a terminal illness.
>
> **Friend.** Oh, that sounds so frightening. What makes you think that?

Fear. I don't know. I just haven't been feeling right
lately. I keep having this thought, *Something is wrong*,
and I think it's coming from my intuition, like I
just know deep down that something is wrong.

Friend. I know how that feels. I sometimes feel that way, too.
But then I try to go a bit deeper and ask if there's anything
else going on that I don't want to look at or feel. Like if there's
anything I'm feeling that I've pushed aside. Has anything
happened lately that has made you feel scared or sad?

Fear. Yes. One of my close friends from
childhood was just diagnosed with a brain
tumor. I don't think she's going to make it.

Friend. Oh, goodness. I'm so sorry. That
sounds so scary and so sad.

Fear (now with some grief). Yes, I feel so sad. I
feel sad for her kids and her husband, and I can
only imagine how scared she must feel.

Silence. A good friend allows for silence
when pure feelings arise.

Fear/Grief. Oh God, I'm so sad for her. And I feel scared for
me, too. What if that happens to me? [This character wants to
dart away from the vulnerability of feeling the pure feeling.]

Friend. As soon as I hear "what if," I know we're in
anxiety territory. I know that's a really scary thought,
but let's come back to the feelings. Can you stay
with the sadness and the vulnerability? Let's put a
hand on your heart. [Places hand on heart.]

Grief/Uncertainty (crying now). I'm just so sad. Life is so uncertain. What can we hang on to? How could this happen to someone so young? What do I do with this?

Friend. You just feel it. Let yourself feel it. Grief is medicine. There's nothing to do but be.

You might be thinking, "I would never know how to say those things to a friend. I'm not that wise, and sometimes I just don't know what to say." You start where you are. You do the best you can with responding to yourself with compassion and curiosity. Remember: when you can shift from a mindset of shame and judgment to one of compassion and curiosity, you're doing the work. So even if you don't know the exact words, it doesn't matter; what matters is that you start to pay close attention to every time you're judging yourself or falling prey to a shame story and are willing to step into a new mindset that is powered by the headlight of curiosity and held in the hand of compassion.

Note: I use the terms wise self/inner parent/compassionate friend interchangeably, and I encourage you to use the one that resonates most strongly for you.

PRACTICE   LOCATE YOUR INNER PARENT/ WISE SELF/COMPASSIONATE FRIEND

Take some time to reflect on and write down any times in your life when you've been able to show up for yourself in a present, attentive, clear way. If it's easier for you to recall a time when you've been a compassionate friend to another, that's okay. Again, the fact that you can do it for someone else means that the capacity and resource lives inside you and simply needs the right attention in order to grow. Remember what it felt like inside when you listened to your friend, what kinds of things you said, how your friend responded. If you can't recall a specific time with a friend, think about how you show up for a pet: how you care for a pet, what sacrifices you make, how you respond when the pet is in pain or seems sad. Anytime you show up for another being with compassion, you are accessing this inner part, which we call the wise self or the compassionate friend. Locating and accessing this part is one of the essential keys to breaking free from anxiety.

The Escape Hatch of Perfection: A Way to Avoid Responsibility

There are so many ways that we can avoid pain and, thus, responsibility. We can choose denial. We can self-medicate with drugs and alcohol. We can fall prey to fear's insidiously convincing beliefs that to turn inward is "selfish, indulgent, and will get you nowhere." We avoid pain because we live in a culture that teaches us to avoid pain. We avoid pain because we don't know that turning toward pain—and I use pain as an umbrella term for anything uncomfortable that we wish to avoid feeling—is one of the secret pathways to joy.

For most people, especially those prone to anxiety, one of the default methods of avoiding pain is to travel up to the safe regions of your mind where pain can't find you. There you sit at the great loom of intrusive thoughts and spin your web of "what ifs" and "if onlys," each thread keeping you stuck in anxiety about the future or regret of the past. Grief can't find you there, lost like the girl in "Rumpelstiltskin," in the uppermost corner of your mental castle, spinning and spinning your golden threads. Except this thread isn't gold. It might shimmer like gold. It might lure you like gold. But there's nothing golden about being stuck in the cold chambers of the mind. Safe, yes. But it's not alive, rich, or full. It's simply where you've learned to go because you haven't been taught another way to tend to pain.

On this loom, alongside thoughts that characterize anxiety—"What if I'm dying?" or "What if I'm in the wrong city?"—escape-hatch threads weave their way into the fabric of the psyche. These sound like, "I'll never be a mother" and "I'll be happy when I [finish this degree; have a baby; find the right partner]." Everyone has escape-hatch threads that are as familiar to their inner landscape as breathing. And almost all these thoughts are braided with the thread of perfection.

It simmers down to one, simple, powerful belief: "If I'm perfect, I'll avoid pain." The sister beliefs are: "If I'm with my perfect partner, I'll avoid pain" or "If I find the perfect [house, city, job], I'll avoid pain."

Embedded in the quest for perfection is the quest for certainty. Ego believes that the attainment of perfection is the safeguard against the uncertainty that defines human life. But of course, perfection is never attained because it doesn't exist. Even if we consciously know this, a part of us rails against this reality and still keeps trying. We create more subtle yet elaborate ways to escape from the messiness and discomfort of being human, from the unavoidable reality that life includes pain, loss, and ultimately, death.

A moment of pain can enter as quietly as a feather landing on the cushion of the heart. One day I was sitting outside, and I had the thought, "I want to move." I know my mind well enough to realize that this had become one of my escape hatches starting with the September 2013 flood here in Colorado that turned our world upside down. I had dabbled with the idea of moving prior to the flood, but after we lost our land and almost lost our house, I experienced a new level of uncertainty that I desperately wanted to avoid again. Now the thought "I want to move" or the image of a picture-perfect house arrived on the heels of a pinprick of pain.

In that moment, instead of attaching onto the thought and indulging it by getting online and searching for a new and "perfect" house (which I've been prone to do), I said out loud, "There's no perfect house." I named the defense, and in doing so, I allowed the grief to surface. Sometimes the grief is connected to a current circumstance, and sometimes it's connected to the nameless grief that runs like an underground river through our human lives. After calling out the fantasy of perfection, I backtracked through my heart to find the source of the pain. *Oh, yes, there it is. Breathe.*

I named; I breathed; I felt. And in the naming and feeling, the top-layer defenses simmered down into a purr of contentment, the place where all experiences and emotions live harmoniously. It's not that I bypassed the pain and found happiness; rather, I made room for the pain at the tea table of my heart and, in doing so, reversed the habitual escape-hatch fantasy of some other perfect house that would lift me out of the pain of being human.

Every time you name your defenses, you drop out of the head-space of anxiety and into the heart-space of the present moment. It's in this space, and through these acts of taking responsibility and embracing life instead of avoiding it, that healing starts.

The Timeline of Healing

As we continue along this path, it's important to name another obstacle that can interfere with healing anxiety: our expectations of the timeline of healing. In our linear, achievement-oriented culture—with a healthy dose of striving for perfection thrown in—we expect that once we read a book or commit to a practice, we will be healed within a few months. But healing doesn't follow the timetable of the culture. It follows the timetable of the soul, which is circular, fluctuating, and mysterious.

We learn and heal in ebbs and flows, spiraling around the center of ourselves where our true self dwells. When we're in a cycle of growth, we burn through layers of ego fears and touch into that core place of wellness where peace and clarity reside. Our hearts are open and alive, and we can receive and give love with ease. This is the gold of being human, and how we long to live there always! But alas, inevitably, when our fear-based self, which often manifests as resistance, senses that we're growing "too much" or learning "too quickly," it bucks like a bull at a rodeo. And suddenly, it feels like we're back at square one. Then we cycle into the ebb stage, and if we don't have a context in which to understand the cycle of healing, the fear-mind can easily grab hold of these ebbs as evidence to support our current anxiety story.

I often receive questions from course members and comments on my website on this topic of relapses or setbacks. However, I don't see them as setbacks as much as times when the fear-based self steps in with greater passion to try to convince you that it's not safe to grow. As I explained, this part of us fears growth because it fears for its life: each time we grow a layer closer to true self, the fear-based self dies a bit. And nobody wants to die—even the parts of our psyche that we can't see or touch.

Because we live in a linear culture, we expect growth to occur linearly. We step onto the healing path and expect the curve to progress upwardly, just like everything else in life (or so the culture teaches). While this may be the path that the culture entrains us to expect—first grade follows kindergarten; second grade follows first grade; baby must follow house purchase must follow marriage—it's not actually how real life goes. In fact, if you look closely, very few things in life progress linearly. We move toward our partner and then we retreat. We feel in touch with a higher presence, in love with our spiritual path, and then doubt sets in. We think we've found our "calling" only to discover a few years into the job that we're ready to do something else.

When you go through a so-called relapse, as you inevitably will, remind yourself that you're ready for the next layer of learning. Remember that apathy is also emptiness, and emptiness is what precedes growth: the stillness of winter, which looks like apathy in its "deadness," is readying the earth for the aliveness of spring. If you can avoid the pitfall of using the emptiness/apathy/numbness as evidence that something about your external life is wrong and instead sit with the emptiness itself without assigning meaning to it, you will find your clarity once again. Clarity doesn't always mean happiness, but it does mean self-responsibility. And that's where our wellness dwells.

4

TRANSITIONS

> In other words, *change* is situational. *Transition*, on
> the other hand, is psychological. It is not those
> events, but rather the inner reorientation and self-
> redefinition that you have to go through in order
> to incorporate any of those changes into your life.
> Without a transition, a change is just a rearrangement
> of the furniture. Unless transition happens, the
> change won't work, because it doesn't "take."
>
> **WILLIAM BRIDGES**
> *Transitions: Making Sense of Life's Changes*

We can't have a thorough discussion of anxiety without talking about transitions. While some people can go with the flow during life's changes, most people experience change as a death experience, which leaves unfinished transitions carrying the seeds for future pain, especially if the grief around the transition wasn't fully processed at the time. Change can be enormously disruptive. Therefore, an important step in healing our anxiety is to undergo transitions consciously and take steps toward repairing the effects of the unhealed transitions from the past.

Transitions are ruptures in the soul, when the earth of our being opens up, and through the fissure, current and old pain emerge. Transitions are potent—full of potential in terms of what can arise. And in this potent state of groundlessness, we have a choice: to seal ourselves up more tightly and calcify the protective casing around the heart, or to yield to the soft feeling that, like a hand reaches up through the cracks, invites us to take hold and heal.

Most people struggle to some degree through the major milestones in life—kindergarten, adolescence, graduating from high school and going away to college, graduating from college, starting a career, getting married, having a baby, buying a house. Those who are more sensitive, because they're acutely aware of the fleeting and ephemeral nature of life punctuated by the fact that loss and death exist, feel the daily death-and-rebirth transitions more acutely than the average person. This means that transitions both small and large—dawn and dusk, anniversaries, the change of seasons, birthdays—need to be honored and acknowledged in order for well-being to exist. While in the midst of change, even if the change is toward something joyous and positive, like a wedding or moving into your dream house, it is normal and healthy to feel: sad, confused, angry, disoriented, scared, terrified, numb, lonely, or vulnerable.

Most people lack basic information about transitions that can help them contextualize these emotions, make sense of them, and move through them effectively. Culturally, we focus on the externals of a transition—planning a wedding, buying the car seat, packing the boxes—to the exclusion of the inner realm. While the externals are important, when we bypass working consciously with the emotions activated during transitions, we decrease our chances of adjusting to the new life as gracefully as possible. This can have long-term, negative consequences not only during the transition at hand, but for our lives in general, and can lead to a buildup of anxiety.

The Three Stages of Transition

Every transition involves passing through three phases:

> **Letting Go.** During which we separate from the
> old life, grieve the losses, express and explore
> fears and expectations about the new life.

In-Between or Liminal. During which we're in the liminal (limbo) zone of transition—detached from the old life but not yet established in the new one—a highly uncomfortable place, characterized by feeling numb, disoriented, depressed, and out of control.

Rebirth. During which we embrace the new life and identity and feel confident, comfortable, and excited about the possibilities of growth that a new beginning holds.

Each day and year, everyone goes through multiple life changes that, with simple information and consciousness, could be transformed from anxiety-inducing and depleting events to life-affirming and transformational experiences. We habitually think of transitions as hard or negative, but most people fail to recognize that embedded in these predictable life-cycle occurrences are opportunities that invite us to spiral into our fears and grief so that we heal at deeper levels each time. Instead of powering through transitions as quickly as possible, we would benefit greatly by embracing them. (After all, we're all in the transition of life, bookended by birth and death; it's just that some transitions stand out in greater relief than others.) Life is ever changing, and when we approach transitions with the intention of growth, we eventually learn how to accept this truth with grace. And, most importantly, when you walk through a transition consciously, you're given a potent opportunity to shed a layer of mindsets, beliefs, patterns, and habits that are contributing to your anxiety.

The Transitions That the Culture Doesn't Talk About

Anxiety festers in the shame that is bred through unrealistic expectations and faulty information. When we respond to the cultural expectation that we shouldn't feel the sadness inherent to the smaller losses in life—the micromoments that few people name and discuss—our inner fields are ready for sowing the seeds of self-doubt and shame. When voiced, this can sound like "Everyone seems so happy about this upcoming holiday weekend, but I feel dread and sadness, so I guess there's something wrong with me," or "I get a pit in my stomach every Sunday night, but I've never heard anyone talk about it, so I guess there's something wrong with me." When the statement "There's something wrong with me" enters your inner dialogue, you're just a few steps away from anxiety ensuing.

As a culture, we desperately need more language about both the obvious and subtle breaking-and-renewing points in our lives. You need to know there will be times, like at the day's end when you peer off the cliff of afternoon into the vast blue sea of twilight, when a great emptiness may arise. The tendency is to run from it—to find something or someone to take it away—but when you know that the emptiness is normal, and you have even a vague sense of why the sadness is there, you can more easily remember to sit and breathe through it until it passes through, and a great fullness is revealed. When we don't know what to expect, we fall into our default modes, which are shame and anxiety.

Let's explore a few of these micromoments so that you can begin to notice and name the many emotions that may be stirred up around them. The first of these—the shifting of light to darkness, of summer to autumn—hits me square in the heart every year. If I don't attend to it directly, it comes back around in the form of anxiety, but when I remember to meet life on life's terms and sink into this annual yet subtle transition, I can continue on in the flow of life.

Loss of Light

Light fading, time passing, big boy is ten, baby isn't a baby, and the time for having babies is over. I see the pregnant woman in the checkout line, and suddenly it's eleven years ago, and I remember being pregnant with my own belly of hope and love, on the threshold of everything new and exciting. There was pain then, too, but now the joy and anticipation come flying to me from past to present—another layer of recognition that a stage of life is over. Oh, this life. Oh, the sensitive soul with the acute awareness of the passage of time and how it just keeps on marching on.

Light fading, time passing, my birthday week. When the passing years are filled with more wisdom and equanimity, why does a birthday bring grief? It's not the birthday itself; it's the transition that a new age can only happen by letting go of the old. There's a birth and a death. It's the law of transitions, of every rite of passage. It's the heart of my work, my deepest passion, and yet every year, I grieve the time change, the loss of an hour of light.

"It's a melancholic time," my husband says. "And beautiful." A strong strain of melancholy runs in his artist's soul. He seems more welcoming of the loss of the light than I do. I find it no coincidence that I was born shortly after the time change. The Jungian analyst Marion Woodman says that we go through transitions much the same way as we come into the world (breach, late, C-section, natural). Perhaps it's also true that our soul's callings are connected to the season in which we were born. I know there are people who welcome the darkness, who feel at home in months that require insulation. I do, too, but it takes me a little while to get there.

"It's a time of loss," my husband says, reminding me of everything I teach. It's the time when old losses filter up to consciousness. The loss of his father. The loss of my grandmother. Her birthday week as well. I miss her. I sense her close now. I see her roses behind my eyelids. I feel the light of her smile when she greets me at the front door. I taste her chopped string beans and barbecue chicken and salad fresh from my grandfather's garden. She was one of my angels, and is still.

I listen to my clients and hear a sad chord of loss for many of them: a grandfather passing; a relationship that didn't bloom; the memories of mothers and fathers that are no longer here. We hold hands through this birth canal, all of us tender human souls that must endure loss as part of our stay on this planet. For those of us who are attuned to transitions, a time change is a portal, and we're squeezing ourselves through it, contorting uncomfortably to the rhythm.

There is one accessible relief for the discomfort. It's the medicine that nature-psyche-soul has given us for loss: grieving. What starts as emptiness as I watch the fading light turns into fullness once the tears drop like rain into my inner well. I cry and write and surrender to what is. There is no fighting nature; the seasons change, and time passes, and no matter what humans exert onto this great, beautiful planet, we will never change the laws of nature. She is teaching us, always, the perfection of her rhythms: that when we surrender and grieve—which means stopping long enough to allow the tears to rise up and release—we are offered an opportunity to tend to the sadness that lives in the heart. It's so easy to run from it during the warm, active seasons of long daylight. These shorter days signal the beginning of the time to turn inward, to snuggle into the sacred and vulnerable places, and allow for the emptiness, the dormant time from which the new seeds for next spring's rebirth will gestate. When we breathe into the darkness instead of running from it, we remember that there is nothing to fear. When we meet it, we transform emptiness into fullness and turn what could be a moment of anxiety into a moment of gold.

Sunday Anxiety

Sunday anxiety is a common experience that strikes many people who struggled with school as children or with work as adults. It's the anxiety that hits when we know we have to show up on Monday for a life that currently triggers anxiety or causes us to recall past anxiety. Years ago, I worked with a client who struggled intensely with this particular anxiety. Instead of acknowledging it directly, she would project it onto the familiar screen of her partner's face and listen to the well-worn song on the track of her psyche called "Not Enough." She would analyze their day *(Were we connected enough?)*, analyze his face *(Cute enough?)*, and analyze herself *(Am I enough?)*. Eventually she was able to recognize this as the hypervigilant part of herself: the part that was scanning the horizon, looking for lurking danger.

As we talked it through, I encouraged her to give her hypervigilant Sunday anxiety a name—the name of someone who had accompanied her through decades of life. Now was the time to invite it out from the shadows and make it real so that it didn't have to make a sideways appearance, demanding attention by banging on the back door and making a ruckus about her lovely husband. Once she had a name for it, I encouraged my client to make a preemptive strike. Instead of waiting for the anxiety to play the "Not Enough" song the next Sunday, invite it in through the front door for conversation. Then she could dialogue with it directly and ask what it was needing. With a loving parent at the helm of the dialogue, did they need to time travel back to those painful Sundays as a child, when school was on the horizon? Did they need to sit on that single bed together, loving parent and young child, while the child told the adult her story and buried her head into an imaginary loving shoulder while she cried? When my client sought out her Sunday anxiety and engaged in a dialogue, she simmered the anxiety down to the core need—needing time and space to revisit past grief and loneliness—and the presenting projection disappeared.

It takes courage to travel into these uncharted waters, which make themselves known in the liminal zone of Sunday evening. It takes courage to trust that you can handle what you find there. It takes courage to become your own friend, the one that can cradle your pain and seek comfort when the pain feels too big to handle alone.

Morning Anxiety

We're all familiar with the term "morning sickness," yet few people discuss another common malady that affects many of us: morning anxiety. My clients and course members who struggle with anxiety often describe waking up in the morning with knots in their stomach, unable to eat, dreading another day of facing their anxious mind. And the common question is: Why? Why does anxiety seem to hit hardest first thing in the morning?

Mornings are the liminal hour, the vulnerable time between night and day when we're in between two states of being: the unconscious, where dreams occur, and the conscious state of our daytime hours. A hallmark of the liminal zone is feeling vulnerable, out of control, disoriented, and uncertain. It's when the bedrock of our familiar life falls away and we're left floating around in the middle of the ocean without a compass or rudder.

Mornings are *yin* (feminine consciousness) time, when our normal defenses soften, and we're offered a portal into the soul. Mornings are soft, fluid, and round. In a healthy mental state, this softness gives rise to creative and spiritual openings and is often when lines of poetry or a creative idea bubble up from the dark, sacred world of psyche. The veils are lifted, and we see things as they are.

When you're in an anxious state, this time offers a window to see the anxiety without the normal distractions of your busy day. In the quiet of morning, the messages of anxiety, which may bang on the doors of your mind during your loud, busy day, now only have to tap lightly for you to listen. Since the habitual response to anxiety is to withdraw and run from it, the mainstream advice for morning anxiety is to get up and get moving. This is, of course, the same message that most people receive about all of their uncomfortable, "negative" feelings: Get over it. Get up. Get moving. Exercise. Take a shower. Get going with your day.

Instead, I urge you to find the courage to walk through the murky portal of the morning hours and explore the anxiety with curiosity as you remind yourself that it carries a message and it's here to teach you something important about yourself. If you try to ignore it, it will only follow you throughout your day in the form of intrusive thoughts and their corresponding physical symptoms. Since you can't escape it, you may as well embrace it.

For as far back as I can remember, a journal has sat on my bedside table, and before my dreams or early-morning musings can take flight and become lost in the sea of my day, I write. When I begin my day by connecting inward and making time for soul, the rest of my day unfolds with more equanimity. Even in the depths of my dark night of the soul throughout my twenties, I would begin and end each day by turning inward in some way. Again, it takes courage to meet these inner realms, especially when anxiety is at the fore. But remember, if you don't meet them lovingly, they will find a way to meet you, often through increasingly alarming intrusive thoughts and other uncomfortable symptoms. When you turn to face your fear instead of waiting for it to catch you, you take one more step in the direction of growing your inner parent and reducing anxiety's grip on your life.

What will your exploration of the anxiety that manifests in the mornings birth for you?

PRACTICE   MEETING WHAT ARISES THROUGH THE FISSURES OF TRANSITIONS

At the beginning or end of the day, after you step away from tablets and phones and people, spend at least five minutes in solitude. Let yourself dwell in the pause, between consciousness and unconsciousness, between masculine and feminine. If you notice longing or sadness travel up to consciousness through the fissure of the transition, consider moving toward it instead of brushing it aside. Notice what thoughts arise in response to the feeling, then gently bring your attention to it as if it were a fairy or a precious gem.

Within this intentional liminal zone, trust where your body wants to lead you. You may want to do some gentle yoga; you may want to dance. You may feel called to sit near an open window and listen to the wind or watch the stars. You may gravitate toward the moon.

If you find yourself face-to-face with the moon, listen to her wisdom. Watch for a poem or painting that may arrive. Trust the feelings that long to emerge. Pay attention to longing. Honor the images that float from unconsciousness to consciousness. Even if you're tired and really "should" get to bed, find a way to express what comes through. Write, paint, dance, breathe, do nothing. Even your silhouette next to the window, drenched in moonlight, is an expression of the divine. Simply being you is enough.

NOTE »

*I'll be following the arc of the
seasons according to the rhythm of
the Northern Hemisphere. If you
live in the Southern Hemisphere,
you'll need to reverse the order.*

5

MONTHS AND SEASONS

Attuning to the Rhythms of the Year

The crickets sang in the grasses. They sang the song
of summer's ending, a sad, monotonous song.
"Summer is over and gone," they sang. "Over and gone,
over and gone. Summer is dying, dying."
  The crickets felt it was their duty to warn
everybody that summertime cannot last forever.
Even on the most beautiful days in the whole year—
the days when summer is changing into fall—the
crickets spread the rumor of sadness and change.

E. B. WHITE
Charlotte's Web

While transitions can be challenging in that they illuminate our stuck places, when we attune to the rhythm of the year, we're not only able to name and process the core feelings of grief or vulnerability as they arise but we're also able to harness the gifts of wisdom that the natural world offers. Anything that helps us align with a deeper rhythm will calm and contain our anxious soul, which longs more than anything else to know that we are safe and to trust that things are being handled. We are animals first and foremost. Yet because of our technological advances and the mounting speed of our culture, we're becoming increasingly cut off from our animal nature and our soul. We're forgetting how to live in alignment with the natural world and the seasons. We're forgetting that nature can aid us on our journey through this life, and that, just like in the great myths of the world, the arc of the seasons is another ally that offers help and clues along the way.

The following diagram will help you visualize the invitation of each season.

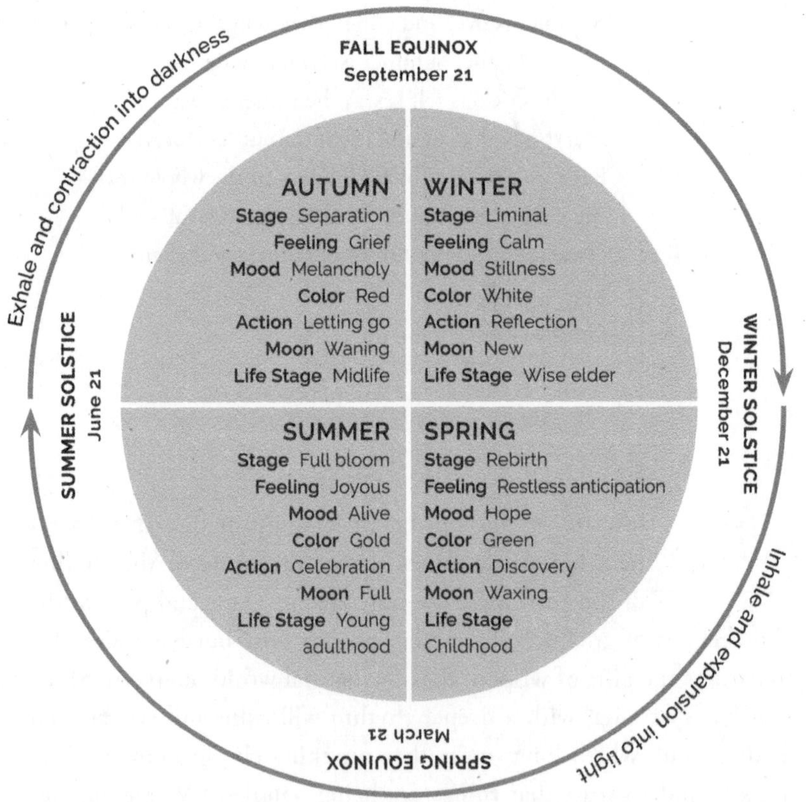

FIGURE 1. SEASONS OF TRANSITIONS

Autumn: The Season of Letting Go

We have all experienced that moment when the scent or feeling of fall arrives on a summer breeze. The air may still be hot with summer's breath, but the winds of change signal that a new season is arriving. Although summer officially begins on June 21, the solstice marks the shift where the days of increasing light turn to days of diminishing light, creating the paradox that characterizes all transitions: just as we are expanding into summer's fullness, we're simultaneously contracting into the shorter days that will reach a decrescendo, when autumn hands the baton to winter. In this sense, autumn has been breathing inside summer's aliveness all along.

Autumn is the quintessential season to illustrate the key features of transitions. Where winter is the season of reflection, spring the season of rebirth, and summer the season of celebration, autumn is the time when we align with the action of nature and ask ourselves the central question of any life transition: "What is it that I need to let go of?" Perhaps it's your habitual thoughts of worry or anxiety; perhaps it's your tendency to nitpick or criticize your partner; perhaps it's getting angry at your kids; perhaps it's the inner critic, the voice that's constantly telling you that you're not good enough. Whatever it is can be blown down to the ground alongside autumn's leaves and decompose into the earth when we choose to focus consciously on what needs to be released.

Autumn is also the time when memory often floods the emotional body. As your kids leave for the first day of school, you may remember those early school days from your own childhood. Whether the memories are positive or negative, you might find yourself pausing for a moment in the bittersweet realm of nostalgia where you become exquisitely aware of the passage of time. Another summer over, another school year beginning, another autumn at your doorstep. If the memory is positive, you might dwell for a few moments in the happy feelings. If the memory is painful, it's an opportunity to allow the feelings to swell up inside you until they bubble into tears and you notice how they roll down your cheeks like the leaves dropping outside.

As the leaves change color and fall, as you sit in front of a crackling fire, as you watch the golden, late-afternoon sunlight cast itself across the yard, ask yourself, "What is it time for me to let go of?" And when the answer appears, throw it into the leaves and the fire and the sunlight and ask for autumn's aid to help you let go.

September Anxiety

The slightly crisp air. The sight of school supplies lining the aisles of the drugstore. The sound of the school bus. Autumn leaves. The loss of light at the day's end. Every year around this time my clients share dreams about showing up at school without any clothes on or forgetting to study for a test.

Why does September bring anxiety? One reason is because it reminds us of school. And, as we discussed in chapter 1, for many people school was a place where their freedom, creativity, love of learning, and social exuberance were clamped down and, quite often, annihilated.

I often think about the one-room schoolhouse my grandparents attended in Upstate New York. Back in the 1920s, school was a luxury, a place where farm children could escape their chores and learn the essential skills that would help them elevate themselves and attend college, which would then secure a career away from the drudgery and physically demanding work of farm life. (I find it interesting and ironic that there's been a "back to the earth" movement in recent years; I wonder what my grandparents would say.) While still dependent on the luck of the draw regarding one's teacher, I imagine that, for the most part, school was an experience that kids looked forward to.

That's not always the case these days. I, for one, loved school through sixth grade, but when I had to change schools in seventh grade, I experienced insomnia for the first time in my life. With the introduction of tests and grades, my genuine love of learning was replaced by the pressure to succeed. Being exposed to social hierarchy and cliques—which seemed largely based on being well dressed—for the first time, my social ease was replaced by the need to please. Where school had once been a place of joy and freedom, it now felt like a prison. September, once an exciting time when I looked forward to clean notebooks and freshly sharpened pencils, was now fraught with dread.

My school experience was a walk in the park compared to what I hear from many of my clients. I'm amazed and heartbroken by how many people who find their way to my work—struggling with anxiety and self-doubt—suffered at the hands of bullies in their school-age years. If I had to give a rough estimate, I would say at least 75 percent of my clients and course members were bullied. Why would this be so? Bullies often target the sensitive, smart, introspective, and introverted kids, which describes my clients to a tee. Perhaps the bullies themselves were highly sensitive babies whose very sensitivity was judged, shamed, and trampled down so early in their life that they couldn't tolerate sensitivity in others. Whatever the cause, when you've been emotionally abused at the hands of your peers, it's very difficult to trust them later in life or even to trust life itself. When your heart has been shattered, it's difficult to believe that it won't shatter again. It's this old pain that you might find arising in early autumn.

Aside from school anxiety, September heralds the change of seasons, and on some level, either consciously or subconsciously, we're attuned to this sense of loss. Here in Colorado we taste the first intimations of autumn's arrival in August. There's a morning chill in the air before the day's heat rises into the nineties. Some of the leaves respond to the shift in temperature and start to turn color. There's an ending, a death, as the season of water and heat descends into colder and darker days. As the world turns inward, psyche follows suit.

The healing response is to turn toward the difficult feelings instead of pushing them away with judgment, shame, resistance, or minimizing. ("Silly self, why are you feeling sad when it's still summer? Nobody else is sad. Get over it.") If grief arises, we breathe into the grief. If a bubble of emptiness hollows the chest, we breathe there as well. If memories of earlier transitions punctuate a moment of day or night, we make room for them and remind ourselves that loss triggers loss, transitions trigger transitions. When we dive fully into the fray of the transition, allowing ourselves to surrender to the feeling of being out of control, vulnerable, and groundless, allowing the tears to flow in response, and transposing the experience into creative expression, we find ground in the underlying and overarching sense that it's all okay.

Winter: Season of Stillness and Gratitude

From the letting go of autumn, we shift into the stillness of winter. This is the quintessential liminal season: no longer grieving but not quite ready to emerge into rebirth. For many people, stillness and solitude are two of the most challenging experiences to endure, and our culture does an excellent job at distracting us from these states. We plan, party, celebrate, consume, and socialize until, on the other side of December, we descend into nothingness. It's here, when the party ends, that the anxiety you were running from has an opportunity to share its wisdom. Listen closely; this is often the time when new patterns, ideas, dreams, and creative projects are born.

Holiday Pain

If you're like most people, there's probably an element of pain, dread and/or overwhelm as you enter the holiday season. The rush to consume, the pressure to feel joyful, and the expectation of experiencing perfect familial bliss set against a Norman Rockwell backdrop is enough to send any human being under a gray cloud. To that, add being a sensitive person who can veer toward anxiety or depression, and the recipe for implosions or explosions is laid out on the holiday table alongside the turkey and cranberries.

The holidays are a setup for disappointment and pain. Whenever we expect to feel a certain way (blissful, connected, happy), the other emotions inside us clamor for attention, until we break down in some form. As discussed in chapter 2, we balk in the face of expectations. And the expectation itself for pure joy is, in a word, ridiculous. Why do we put so much pressure on ourselves to feel one way just because of a calendar date? We treat ourselves like robots that can turn on certain feelings and turn off others just because it's Thanksgiving or Christmas or Hanukkah. Then, because we don't honor it consciously, the inherent pain around holidays and transitions sneaks and sidles through the back door into psyche, and we find ourselves picking a fight with our best friend or crumbling into anxiety or depression.

Every human being carries pain and heartbreak in some form, and it's latent pain that simmers to the surface during the holidays. For some, it's the pain of their own divorce that has shattered their intact family and sends themselves and their kids into preholiday stress, loneliness, and overwhelm. For others, it's the pain of their parents' divorce that sends the now-adult children into separation and distance as they try to navigate blended-family stress. For others, it's the heartbreak of a recent breakup. For still others, it's the grief of having no family or partner at all with whom to celebrate. I could write on and on. The point is: nobody is living the Hollywood *Father of the Bride* dream where pain is airbrushed out to reveal only the perfect house with the perfect family and the perfect life. *It simply does not exist.*

The most challenging part of inviting pain to our holiday season is that we believe the pain shouldn't be there. If you don't even believe it exists, how can you send it an invitation? We carry a fantasy about everyone else's bliss (and social media surely doesn't help in this regard), so that when pain in any form arises (disappointment, loneliness, frustration, sadness), the knee-jerk response is to kick it out the door with a doggy bag of shame for the road. This sounds like: "What's wrong with me? I should have it all together. I have no reason to feel sad." As soon as the healthy and understandable pain is met with shame, the pain quickly morphs into anxiety. In order to head anxiety off at the pass, we have to be willing to feel the raw pain.

PRACTICE   INVITE PAIN
TO YOUR HOLIDAY TABLE

Next time the holidays approach, set aside time to sit down with your journal and allow yourself to write about how you're feeling. Invite your pain to the preholiday gathering. Scoot aside for disappointment. Pull the throne over for heartbreak. You may actually want to create handwritten invitations addressed to Grief, Disappointment, and Heartbreak. Place them in a homemade mailbox created specifically for them. Anytime we can ritualize our feelings, they move through more quickly. As you invite these states inside, write about any memories, stories, images, or sensations that arise; then put your pen aside to allow your body's pain to simmer up to your heart and eyes where you can have a good, big, full-bodied cry. In this way, you will connect to the raw and human feelings that the holidays evoke. In doing so, anxiety will step aside, and you'll make room for genuine joy and gratitude to arrive at the table as well.

The Holy Days: An Opportunity for Gratitude

There's a vulnerability on the planet during the holiday season. I see it in people's faces: beneath the stress and tightness and frantic pace lives the softness of an open heart, as if the emissaries of grief travel from broken heart to eyes and soften the edges. I see the longing for connection, the most basic human desire to break through our isolation and sit comfortably in others' company. I see the desire for peace. I see the longing for love.

It happens in small moments as I walk through my day during the holiday season. I catch the eyes of a driver in the parking lot and smile. She smiles back. A meeting of strangers. I drive out of the parking lot and wave at the homeless man on the corner. "Can we give him anything, Mommy?" my son asks. I know I don't have any small bills. I reach into my wallet and hand my son a large bill, and he rolls down his window and hands it to the man. The man sees the bill, chokes up, and turns away, then turns back to stammer through tears, "God bless you." I put my hand on my heart, and my eyes fill with tears, too. I turn back to look at my son to see his smile radiating as big as his soul. A holy moment.

These small moments of pared-down, openhearted contact are what this season is about. We call these days holidays, but they're also holy days, for embedded in them is an invitation to connect more strongly to peace and love. We can focus on the overconsumption that seems to intensify each year, or we can focus on the archetypal under-pinning that informs every holy day: the desire to connect to our true nature, our essential goodness, and to give from that place to others. To me, that's holiness. It's the unencumbered heart. It's the moments in life when we touch into the divine, which means the highest parts of ourselves that carry a spark of divinity. It can occur at the top of a mountain or on a city street corner. It's when our hearts are wide, wide open—open enough to receive what Martin Buber called the "I-Thou" experiences: standing eye to eye with a person, an animal, a tree, a rock. It's letting ourselves see and be seen without inhibition or obstruction. It is, in a word, love.

That's what this season is about. That's what it means to sink down into the underground river that informs the holidays and turn them into holy days. It's about giving for the pure joy of giving. When you connect with the archetypal river that hums beneath the frantic, anxiety-ridden top-layer pulse of shopping and parties and spending and wrapping, you're given an opportunity to learn more about what it truly means to love.

One of the most giving acts we can engage in is to see another's essence. When we hold another's gaze and see them with eyes of love, we're giving a great gift. I find it fascinating, although not surprising, that many people who find my work are in helping professions: thera-pists, teachers, nurses, doctors, social workers, and, of course, parents. These are people whose hearts are as big as the moon and can easily give to others and see their essences but have a hard time seeing it in themselves. So we start there. We make a prayer during this veil-thin-ning time, when the earth is tilting on its axis and turning into winter: "Please, help me see my goodness. Please let me know that I am loved."

From that filled-up place, even if you remember your goodness for just one moment, you can set your compass to the dial of giving, and your anxiety will diminish. It's important to know that giving doesn't hinge on healing. The ego's common line says, "If I'm not fully healed then how I can give?" The giving facilitates the healing, and the healing nourishes the giving. They work in tandem: twin, symbiotic poles that help us grow and move more and more toward love. And the more love we grow, the less room there is for fear.

Here again is the invitation of this season: to give. We focus on giving gifts, but what if we widened that focus to include giving our hearts? One tangible way to practice this is to set an intention that with every person you meet from now through the New Year—from intimate loved ones to perfect strangers—you will take a moment to see their essential goodness. I once read about a rabbi who would silently say *tehora hee* ("your soul is good") to each person he met. It's similar to what we say at the end of yoga practice: *Namaste*, which means "the light in me sees the light in you." Isn't this what Jesus taught as well—to love your neighbor as yourself? Isn't that what we're celebrating as we walk toward Christmas—the birth of a man who embodied unconditional love and brought peace to this planet? What would it be like to bring this Christ-consciousness into our hearts and make it a conscious practice of seeing goodness and giving this silent or verbal reflection to any life we touch in any form? To see with the spiritual eyes that reside in your heart.

I see you. I see your goodness. I see your heart. I don't know what stories and experiences brought you to this moment in your life, but as I hand you this bill, I'm handing you more than money: I'm handing you a moment of love. We are two humans, each suffering in our own way, each touching into the divine in our own way. As I write this, I'm holding you in my heart. I'm sending you love. I hope you have a warm place to stay tonight. I hope you have a blanket. I hope you have food. I hope my thoughts reach you in some mysterious way. I hope for a more peaceful planet where all beings are free and safe and loved.

If each person oriented their compass in the direction of seeing others' essences, the planet we live on would be different. Perhaps we can view that planet during the window of the holidays by seeing good, reflecting essence, and sending prayers for peace into each heart we meet.

There are two rivers that pulse through the holiday season: a river of anxiety informed by the need to consume and socialize and stay loud and busy, and a river of love informed by the waters of giving and gratitude. The more you choose to connect with the great expansive river of love that pulses beneath and around and between all of us, the more you open your heart and edge out anxiety. In doing so, you will transform the holidays back into holy days.

Listen for the Seed

Winter is often an emotionally challenging time. In the darker months with shorter days, psyche invites us to slow down and dip into her underworld where we find unshed tears, unexplored fears, and latent dreams. We can avoid our shadow during the long days of summer with endless fun-filled distractions, but when autumn then winter settle in, past the rush and glitter of presents and parties, when the long, long month of January unfolds into February's silence, there's no place else to turn but inside. And if we don't have a steady relationship to our emotional life, what our culture calls depression can easily set in.

Depression has many meanings. From a Jungian perspective, depression is the soul's call to sit still and become comfortable with the waiting and nothingness that define the liminal—or in-between—zone. From the perspective of transitions, winter depression is what necessarily follows the high of summer. What goes up must come down, and when we make room for this truth of life, we can stop fighting the archetypal energy that is so present during these months, and instead breathe into the stillness and perhaps discover the gifts that lay wrapped inside. Every time we align with *what is* instead of the expectation of how we think it should be, anxiety has less room to take hold.

When we drop into stillness with reverence and curiosity, we may be surprised at what we find. Yes, there may be wells of tears that need to be shed. There may be loneliness and uncertainty, vulnerability and the fear of the unknown. But there's also something glimmering underneath the winter snows, a seed of creativity, a moment of possibility that, when given attention, can be nurtured into something new: a poem, a story, a project, a recipe, a dance, a song, a painting.

It's not ready to blossom into the fullness of its manifestation, but the tiny beginning is here, and you can only hear it if you slow down enough to listen.

I invite you in winter to listen for the seeds that want to gestate. Listen for the slight vibration of "yes" energy that longs to create new life. There's an archetypal energy embedded in winter, especially February, as it's the month that precedes spring. The sap is starting to quicken. The animals, while still deep in stillness or slumber, are sensing that the first warm wind is close. The crocuses are centimeters away from poking their purple heads above ground. What is vibrating inside of you? What small creative impulse is taking root, ready to begin its journey down the birth canal of psyche and emerge, one day, as something new and alive that will be birthed into this world?

Spring: The Season of Rebirth

On the threshold of spring, we begin to notice a quiet awakening within. The intentions that we set during the dark days of winter may have lain dormant these past months, but now we see the first green heads pushing through and realize that the dawn of something new is upon us. Spring is the season of hope and renewal when, encouraged by the increase of light and warmth, we find the energy to take the necessary action that can push the tentative new beginning into full awakening.

Now is the time to ask yourself: "What is longing to be born? If I set intentions on New Year's Eve, how can I draw upon the energy of renewal and call those intentions into action? What seeds of new beginnings were resting in the underground caverns of my mind and are now bursting into fruition?" Spring is an excellent time to harness the powerful energy of rebirth that surrounds you, to set your intention to burn through a layer of resistance that may be holding you back from your healing.

Sometimes simply noticing the change of seasons is enough to facilitate an inner change. For example, last year I was counseling a mother of two girls. The younger girl enthusiastically threw herself into every new activity and seemed to exhibit little struggle with life. The older one, on the other hand, was more cautious and sensitive, and had been struggling the previous summer with mastering the skill of riding a bike. The girl wanted desperately to ride a bike and join her neighborhood friends in their fun, but something was holding her back.

As spring neared, and the weather warmed, my client and I discussed saying to her daughter, "Spring is here to help you learn this new skill. Just like the first crocuses that bravely show their heads even when the threat of winter is still near, you can find the courage to try to ride your bike again, even when you're scared. Perhaps you just weren't ready last summer. I think you're ready now. What do you think?" The girl said yes, she was ready, and yes, she was still scared. Mother and daughter then planned a special hike together in the early days of spring to observe the ways in which the season was birthing herself. They noticed the tiny green buds on the trees and the delicate blades of wild grasses popping up across the hillsides. They hiked for a few miles, then rested on the earth and felt the warm sun on their faces. When they returned home, the girl rode her bike alone for the first time.

If winter was a season of sorrow, allow the light winds of spring to wash away the residue of grief. If winter was a season of sickness, let the freshness of spring restore you to health. If winter was a season of loss, notice the new life and rebirths that surround you. If winter was a season of silence, invite the birds of spring to bring song back into your life. If winter was a season of hopelessness, connect to the perennial signs of hope that rise up in the natural world as if to say, "Today is a new day. Today I can start something new and find that place of beginning within. Today I am alive and for that I am grateful. Today I see love manifest in the miracles of nature and I whisper a quiet but certain 'Yes.'"

The Restlessness of Spring

Every spring, there's a restlessness in the air. I feel it in the trees, their stored winter sap pulsing to birth their new buds and leaves. I see it in my clients as they wiggle out of the identity that no longer fits—as single person, as nonparent, as employee at a job that no longer serves them. I sense it in many creative people around me who are working to complete the final stages of a project that they've wanted to release into the world for years. I recognize it in myself as I strive to find the balance that seems to perpetually elude mothers. And I witness it in my sons, their whole beings itching in a constant state of discomfort as they reach for the next stage of growth.

During autumn, the invitation from nature is to turn inward as we prepare, like the trees that shed their leaves, to release that which no longer serves us. But during spring, the seasonal counterpoint of autumn, we're also invited to observe the stagnant places revealed through winter's hibernation and let them go. It's a different letting go than happens during fall, not a full shedding as much as a recognition that a new stage is just within reach, and in order to embrace it, we must pass through an uncomfortable "itchy" stage as a layer of skin falls away. The outer world is on the threshold of bursting into the full bloom and celebration of summer; if we look carefully, we'll see that our inner world is also in this simultaneously uncomfortable and exciting state of anticipation.

Sometimes the restlessness is a call to action: we assess the situation at hand and see if there are other possibilities asking to be discovered. But sometimes our tendency to do and solve and fix prevents us from simply witnessing the restlessness and trusting that through this witnessing the new birth will naturally arise.

Summer: The Season of Celebration

Summer is the season of simple and timeless joys. She frolics like a happy child between innocent spring and melancholy autumn, waiting for us to embrace her unbridled delight with life. It's the season when we walk barefoot in the grass; we watch kids run through sprinklers and throw themselves with careless abandon onto Slip 'N Slides; and we wear straw hats, sundresses, and sandals, while eating a single scoop of vanilla ice cream in a wafer cone.

One summer many years ago when my boys were young, my older son and I wordlessly agreed to a daily ritual. After his younger brother fell asleep for his nap, we grabbed our sun hats and each other's hands and walked out to the garden. No matter how much frustration or irritation had pockmarked our morning, as soon as we stepped onto the stones that marked our garden's edge, we exhaled more deeply and felt the tensions dissolve.

Away from computers, phones, and the mounting collection of "kid stuff" that was filling our house, we fell into an easy rhythm as we engaged in the simplest of tasks: weeding, watering, harvesting. The waterfall of words that normally tumbled from his six-year-old lips slowed down, as if his thoughts were following the cadence of his actions. There was space to hear birdsong and the rush of the creek. There was time to bend down low and observe the honeybee drying her tattered wings in the heat of the midday sun.

After my son picked pocketfuls of snap peas, we walked back indoors, sat together on the wicker chair in the screened-in porch, and marveled at the miracle of these delicious green treasures. "Better than candy," he would say, as he thoroughly enjoyed the sweetness of the peas we had planted together in early spring. So simple and so complete. It was, without a doubt, the high point of each day.

The secret is in slowing down long enough to notice the small miracles that surround us, the singular moments of life that can, when we take the time to see them, connect us to a profound sense of joy and gratitude. It can sometimes feel like a Herculean effort to peel ourselves away from the magnetic force of screens and the things we have to do (the ever-growing and never-ending to-do list), but it's an inarguable truth that the simple joys of summer will not be found in that virtual reality or in checking items off the list.

In this culture that exalts technology, achievement, and efficiency to a godlike realm, pushing us into a frantic pace that exacerbates anxiety, we have to listen closely for the simple activities that invite us to slow down to a natural pace. These moments are medicine for the anxious mind; they're what the soul longs for. And summer abounds with these opportunities. It might be as simple as stretching out under a tree, like a cat in the shade, and allowing yourself to unwind in the late-afternoon, languid heat. It might be taking ten minutes in the middle of a workday to sit on a park bench, bite into a crunchy red apple, and notice the shapes of the clouds as they billow across the sky. Do you remember, as a kid, finding dinosaurs and dogs hiding in the clouds? During this childlike season, we can become like children and remember that it's the simple moments and the timeless pastimes that inspire the most joy.

PRACTICE INVITATION OF THE SEASONS

When we align ourselves with the primary action of each season, we can harness the energy that permeates the natural world and, thus, facilitate our own transitions. With each season, take time to journal on the following questions:

- During autumn, as you witness the falling of leaves, I invite you to open to the energy of shedding and ask yourself, "What is it time to let go of?"

- In winter, as you watch the stillness settle over the land and notice the hibernation of your own soul, you can ask, "What arises in quiet and solitude?"

- In spring, the literal and metaphoric seeds that lay dormant for several months tentatively poke their heads through the warming earth, then burst into full bloom, and you can ask, "What is ready to be born?"

- And in summer, as you celebrate the fruits of your labor and enjoy the days of water and sunshine, you can ask yourself, "What is it time to celebrate?"

6

THE VULNERABILITY
OF BEING PRESENT

Bodhichitta is our heart—our wounded, softened
heart. Now, if you look for that soft heart that we
guard so carefully—if you decide that you're going
to do a scientific exploration under the microscope
and try to find that heart—you won't find it. You can
look, but all you'll find is some kind of tenderness.
There isn't anything that you can cut out and put
under the microscope. There isn't anything that you
can dissect or grasp. The more you look, the more
you find just a feeling of tenderness tinged with some
kind of sadness. This sadness is not about somebody
mistreating us. This is inherent sadness, unconditioned
sadness. It has part of our birthright, a family heirloom.
It's been called the genuine heart of sadness.

PEMA CHÖDRÖN
Start Where You Are

We are not taught to meet life on life's terms, that is, living
in the present moment. Left to ourselves, our ego will
shift and move and invent and convince in order to
protect us from meeting life square in the eye. All the ego's intrusive
thoughts and fear-based schemes are, in fact, finely crafted and often
convincing escape hatches designed to remove us from touching the

raw places that define being human—our loneliness, pain, fear, uncertainty, and transcendence—the places that only arise when we drop down into this moment.

One of anxiety's most brilliant defense tactics to protect us from the vulnerability of being present is to lure us into the mind trap of perseverating on the past in the form of regret, guilt, or shame, or of launching us off in the rocket ship of the future where we worry about things that are out of our hands. One of the keys to healing from anxiety is to learn to come into this moment, where our vulnerability lives. This isn't easy, especially since very few people were taught how to tend to vulnerability. In fact, we're taught just the opposite, and often receive the message never to make ourselves vulnerable because it's not safe. This mindset likely made sense for most of our history as humans when it truly wasn't safe to be vulnerable, but as we're at a threshold of consciousness, we're being invited to learn a new way. Anxiety is the guide. Curiosity and compassion are the allies. Being willing to open to the full, raw, tender experience of being human is the light in the darkness.

No Escape Hatch from Life

Alongside our past- or future-based worry, we also use the myth of "I'll be happy when . . ." as an escape hatch. We fall prey to the insidious cultural message that says, "You'll be happy when [you graduate from college, land the job, get married, buy the house, get the dog, have the baby]." or "You'll be happy when [this test is over, this job assignment is complete, the sun comes out]." But when each of those milestones or events occurs, and you still feel restless and uncertain, you wonder what's wrong. There's nothing wrong. It's just that there's no escape hatch from life, meaning we can't avoid the inherent loneliness, pain, uncertainty, and transcendence of being human. Let's explore some of these states a bit further.

Life can be a *lonely* journey. In fact, loneliness is part of the human experience, for it's an undeniable fact that nobody, no matter how close they may come to our hearts, is living inside of our bodies and seeing life through our lens. One of the hidden diamonds embedded inside the questions that often plague the anxious mind is the invitation to embrace our fundamental, existential loneliness. When we're hooked on the questions, we're fixated on the ego's convincing escape hatch that says, "You wouldn't feel lonely with someone else or somewhere else." When we recognize, on the other hand, that loneliness is part of the human condition, we can learn to meet our solitude and, perhaps, even become friends with it. When we meet the solitude instead of running from it, it changes, paradoxically, into friendship—but it's our own internal friendship instead of that of expecting another to fill that place of longing. (We will explore loneliness in more depth in chapter 10.)

Life can be a *painful* journey. For some, especially those with a wide-open heart, pain is a part of daily life. We don't even have to know why we're crying, but when we slow down and soften, we find that a layer of sadness sits in the middle of an open heart. We try to escape this "genuine heart of sadness," as Pema Chödrön describes it, but there's no escape, because life includes pain. If you're someone whose heart hasn't been hardened over, you will be highly attuned to this pain on a daily, and sometimes hourly, basis. *There's no getting over life*; we must learn to go through it.

Life can be a *transcendent* journey: moments, minutes perhaps, when the soul expands, when not just the physical body breathes a full breath, extending beyond the familiar boundaries, but the soul does as well. Transcendence is when the soul recognizes itself, when the infinite part of me remembers itself by seeing itself reflected somewhere in this finite world. The quest for transcendent experiences is not a way to bypass the inherently uncomfortable fact of being a human in a physical body. But we can seek transcendence as we seek oxygen, for these moments in time where we are simultaneously lifted out of ourselves and are remembering ourselves oxygenate our souls and make life worth living.

Where do we find transcendence? There is no formula. We find it by following the faint whispers of *yes* until the quiet song awakens into full chorus, until the transcendent moments aren't isolated experiences, but mark out daily and even hourly life. This may happen when you're hiking in the hills, sitting in prayer, looking at art, writing a poem or memorizing one, working with a dream, climbing a mountain, sitting on the beach, or petting a cat. We leap from lily pad to lily pad of *yes* until they string together to create one green path that guides our days and nights.

We must make space and call on the ally of slowing down into stillness to invite the *yes*. We must carve out a quiet spot in some corner of our busy lives to hear the insects singing. And we must know that transcendence is not the goal and is not, in fact, separate from the pain and loneliness, the fear and vulnerability that define being human.

Transcendence is meeting life on life's terms, putting down the armor, stopping the fight, and simply saying, "Here I am. I allow life to flow through me and with me. I say yes to life in all of its varied expressions of pain and beauty. Here I am."

The Fear of Feeling Too Good

As much as we yearn for transcendence, we also resist it, for it's just as vulnerable to feel good as it is to struggle. In fact, in many ways it's *more* vulnerable to feel good, because when you're feeling good, you have something to lose, and the ego fears nothing more than loss. Therefore, in order to learn to say yes more often to the vulnerability of life in the present moment, we need to explore the natural resistance that arises when we're feeling good.

You long to feel better. You're sick of suffering. But when goodness arises, you notice a thought process that pushes it away with something like, "I don't deserve to be happy," or "If I'm happy, something will come to take it away." This is your defense system at work, your ego working overtime to protect you from the risk of being vulnerable. Because it's as much of a risk to feel good as it is to feel pain. The only safe zone is the narrow place where feelings are muted into a manageable, numb place. This is the place that our neck-up (always in our heads) culture teaches. The path to freedom is to learn to peel back the protective layers that have kept you safe until now, and risk touching life directly again.

One of my course members described it like this:

> I have entire days without experiencing anxiety, and
> everything feels so real—it's as if I had been wearing
> gloves all my life and can suddenly touch the texture,
> shape and temperature of my emotions, and of life in
> general. Every moment feels very real when it's not covered
> by the thick layer of anxiety and constant worries.
>
> When I am in this space, though, I sometimes feel
> very scared and actually do get very anxious. I am afraid
> something bad will happen. I feel I don't deserve to be
> happy, to be content with my partner and my job, despite
> all the imperfections. I am uncovering this deep belief that
> it is dangerous to be happy. Any guidance on how to deal
> with this fear?

If this description sounds familiar, you're not alone. You're suffering
from what Gay Hendricks, in his book *The Big Leap*, names the Upper
Limit Problem. Here he shares his own process of discovering this
phenomenon:

> I had just returned to my office from lunch with a friend,
> and we'd spent a congenial hour talking about the projects
> we were working on. My work was going well, and I was
> happy in my relationships. I leaned back in my chair and
> gave myself a good stretch, letting out a sign of relaxed
> satisfaction. I felt great. A few seconds later, though, I
> found myself worrying about my daughter, Amanda,
> who was away from home on a summer program she
> has very much wanted to attend. A slide show of painful
> images flickered through my mind: Amanda sitting alone
> in a dorm room, Amanda feeling lonely and miserable
> away from home, Amanda being taunted by other kids.
> The inner joy disappeared from my body as my mind
> continued to produce this stream of images.

He then calls the program director and learns that his daughter is fine. He feels foolish and wonders how he could go from feeling good in one moment, then watching the slideshow of painful images in the next. Then he realizes that his mind sent him the painful images *because* he was feeling good. As he says, "Some part of me was afraid of enjoying positive energy for any extended period of time. When I reached my Upper Limit of how much positive feeling I could handle, I created a series of unpleasant thoughts to deflate me."

Sound familiar? Let's deconstruct the belief that it's not safe to be happy.

I always like to zoom out to start at the biggest layer of a belief, which in this case resides in the collective unconscious. Remember the collective unconscious is the part of the mind that is shared by all humans and is even connected to the memory of our ancestors. In other words, we often believe that we're the only ones to experience or feel something, but when we zoom out and connect to the invisible web, we see that our personal experience is also the collective experience. Gay Hendricks describes how the fear of feeling too good is interwoven into the collective layer, how human beings have struggled through adversity for thousands of years, and that it's only recently that we have evolved to allow ourselves to feel good for any length of time.

Of course, not everyone on the planet is blessed enough to worry about life being too good. There are millions of people who suffer on the most basic level of survival. The fear of feeling too good, while collective for many, isn't universal, and would be categorized in Maslow's hierarchy of needs in the very top tier: self-actualization. This doesn't invalidate how painful and self-limiting it can be when you're suffering from the fear of feeling too good, but I do believe it's important to approach that fear with a healthy dose of perspective.

The next layer to address is the level of ego. Again, the ego is committed to one thing above all else: avoiding loss by maintaining control. In pursuit of this futile quest for ultimate control, it convinces us that if we believe its lies, we will successfully control the future. In this case, the ego says: "If you acknowledge the good things in your life, you'll make them go away." Can you hear the magical thinking in that statement?

And finally, we address the personal story, times when you were torn down by peers, teachers, siblings, or parents for shining your light brightly. I can still remember the cliquey girls in fifth grade saying to me about another girl, "She's so conceited," or "She thinks she's so great," with great disdain. For a young child for whom peer acceptance is the entire world, it's a small leap from hearing those statements spoken about someone else, to then introjecting them into one's own code. In that one moment, we learn to remain small.

In the end, it's about recognizing, over and over again, where you have control and where you don't. You can't control the future; you can't control the outcome of most events in your life. But you can control how you choose to respond to the fear-based, what-if thoughts that descend on your mind like an avalanche and try to pull you away from this moment, right here, right now. You can control how you respond to your inner world and how much responsibility you're willing to take for your well-being. This is what you'll learn in the next practice.

PRACTICE WORKING WITH THE FEAR OF FEELING TOO GOOD

When you're noticing that the fear of feeling too good is in the picture, use the following practice:

1. **Notice it.** Bring awareness to times when your good feelings suddenly shift into worry and rumination. The more consciousness you bring to this habit, the more easily you'll be able to change it.

2. **List your ego's beliefs and call them to the mat.** The ego is most powerful when it works in darkness, hidden behind the great Oz curtain. When you pull back the curtain, you discover that the ego, just like

the wizard of Oz, isn't a big, scary person with a loud voice, but is actually just a small, little, scared part of us. When you write down all of your ego-beliefs, you shine the light of consciousness on them, and they begin to dissolve.

3. **Write or explore times in your life when you've been torn down by others.** Or write about experiences that led to the belief that it's not safe to be fully, extraordinarily, beautifully, magnificently, brilliantly you. Most people learn somewhere along the way that it's not okay to think they're wonderful and that it's safer to stay small. When you explore these experiences, you release them from your individual unconscious and can bring truth to the beliefs that were formed during those times. Grief may also surface as you come into direct contact with memories in which you were made to feel small, especially when those memories are connected to your parents.

4. **Name your fears.** Write down what scares you about doing inner work that might result in feeling more grounded and joyful. When you've spent years or decades identified with your pain and anxiety, it can feel scary to imagine a new identity, one based on feeling well. Most people resist committing to their inner world because they're scared of what they'll find.

It is essential to take your inner work slowly and with great gentleness. You are likely fused with your core stories, like a tenacious weed that has wrapped itself around your core self: if you pulled out the weed by the root too quickly, it would feel like your core self was collapsing. Since you've lived with your stories and beliefs for so long, it's part of the internal structure or building block of your psyche. Like a gentle gardener, the work has to be slow and methodical, perhaps pulling out the top portion of the unwanted weedy vine before carefully digging into the ground to unearth the root.

When ego tries to scare you with one of its favorite lines ("If you commit to inner work and grow, something bad will happen, or you'll find out something terrible about yourself."), it's also essential to grab onto a bit of cognitive truth and know that what you'll find is yourself. What you'll learn is how to love, both yourself and others. What you'll realize is that unattended anxiety takes up a tremendous amount of space, and then when you begin to dissolve its tentacles, your heart will open in untold ways. In short, nothing bad will come from doing your inner work; that's the ego's fear of change at work, trying to convince you to leave well enough alone and act like everything's fine. If anxiety is in charge, everything is *not* fine. And the more you turn inward and find the courage to come face-to-face with your raw spots that live in the vulnerability of the present moment, the more you will find your freedom.

PART TWO

THE FOUR REALMS OF SELF

Healing Anxiety from the Ground Up

We need to learn to take a walk in the sunshine
and see the colors of the earth, to respect our
physical bodies, to wake up to the music in
life, to listen to our dreams, to show affection to
the people we love. Then we can make peace.

ROBERT JOHNSON
We: Understanding the Psychology of Romantic Love

7

THE SEAT AT THE HEAD
OF YOUR TABLE

> Self-actualization is not a sudden happening or even the
> permanent result of long effort. The eleventh-century
> Tibetan Buddhist poet-saint Milarepa suggested: "Do
> not expect full realization; simply practice every day of
> your life." A healthy person is not perfect but perfectible,
> not a done deal but a work in progress. Staying
> healthy takes discipline, work, and patience, which is
> why our life is a journey and perforce a heroic one.
>
> DAVID RICHO
> *How to Be an Adult in Relationships: The Five Keys to Mindful Loving*

In order to meet the essential task of attending to your four realms of self, you need to have a loving, competent, and clear inner parent or inner friend at the helm of psyche. Just as kids feel safe when there's an attuned parent sitting at the head of the meta-phoric dinner table, so your inner characters—Anxiety, Judgment, Fear, Jealousy, Critic, Taskmaster, Good Girl/Boy—feel safe when there's a loving, clear, attuned parent at the head of your inner table. Neglecting this one essential quality of self can lead to more anxiety, overwhelm, and confusion, especially when engaging in deep inner work. Whereas growing the quality will allow you to meet your body, heart, mind, and soul in ways that allow you to listen to and act on anxiety's messages.

The Qualities of a Loving Inner Parent

We *all* have this calm, compassionate place inside us, but if you didn't witness emotional regulation role-modeled when you were growing up (and very few people did), it can be difficult to access it. This doesn't mean that this part of you doesn't exist. (Remember: one of the favorite tactics of the character of resistance is to tell you that you don't have a loving inner parent, and therefore can't do this inner work.) It just means that this part is a weak muscle inside you that needs your attention in order to strengthen it. To do so, it can be helpful to know which qualities you're looking for, so that when you notice them, you can say, "Yes, there's my inner parent." Whatever you water will grow, and in this case, you want to grow a particular part of you that can hold steady when life swirls around you and as you dive more deeply into your inner world and healing process. Following are some basic qualities of a loving inner parent.

- Just as a loving outer parent listens to and honors a child's needs yet pushes them past their comfort zone when necessary, so a loving inner parent brings compassion and intense curiosity to your inner world while making sure that you don't fall into the realm of indulgent pain or laziness.

- Just as a loving outer parent carves out time to drop down into the present moment and connect eye to eye and heart to heart with their child without distraction, so the inner parent recognizes how essential it is to create long pauses in the otherwise run-on sentence of our increasingly fast and busy days so that she or he can listen with full presence to what's needed. This means that phones are turned off or placed in another room. It means that we hush the voices—the work, the calls, the emails, the bills—that pull us away from the dropped-down time of presence. We cannot feel safe, loved, or worthy if the parents in our lives—both outer and inner—don't take time to listen.

- In addition to being a listener and holder, the loving, wise parent is the part of ourselves that sets boundaries and limits. It's the part that says yes to this ("Yes, I'm going to exercise now even though I don't feel like it") and no to that ("No, I'm not going to drink alcohol tonight, because I know it will cause me to wake up feeling anxious tomorrow"). It's the part that can make decisions and trust those decisions.

- When you have a loving parent at the head of the table, you can feel your difficult feelings—sadness, jealousy, disappointment, anger, frustration, loneliness, boredom—without being swallowed by them. You also learn that you don't have to believe every thought that parades through your mind. And just because you have a thought, it doesn't mean you will act on it. When you trust that you have an adult at the head of the table, you know that your thoughts are simply thoughts and that there's a cavernous divide between thoughts and actions.

- The loving parent validates the courage it takes to commit to inner work and reminds you quite often, sometimes several times a day, that to heal from the root requires patience, skill, and trust. Our fast-food, quick-fix, instant-gratification culture is eroding our capacity for accessing patience. In our warped sense of time, we expect relief *now*. We've lost our appreciation for slow-cooked experiences, from literal food to the emotional realm of soul. We no longer write letters and wait with anticipation for a response. We've nearly lost our capacity to *be* in any regard, from sitting by a fire with no sound other than the crackling of the flames to lying in the grass and staring out at the sky without a phone by our side.

There is no way to rush healing. The soul, like animals, continues to move at its own pace, according to its own rhythm. This is a source of frustration to our modern minds, which have forgotten how to wait, but it's the loving inner parent's task to remind you to shift your focus a few degrees and slip into a new context, one that understands slow living and slow healing. In the space of patience, you will find a place to exhale.

PRACTICE GROWING YOUR WISE SELF/INNER PARENT

Your wise self is like a muscle, and the more you use it, the stronger it becomes. Every time you consciously recognize that you acted from a place of clarity and wisdom, your inner parent becomes stronger. In fact, it's the recognition itself that strengthens this muscle, for just as kids need their caregivers and mentors to witness and acknowledge their intrinsic gifts and strengths, so our inner characters need to be acknowledged. Every time you engage in inner work of any kind, you strengthen your inner parent. Every time you exercise even when you don't feel like it or move toward your partner despite the fear-walls that try to keep you separate, the inner parent grows stronger.

A concrete exercise that can grow your inner parent is to begin to regularly and consciously name the other characters in your psyche that vie for the seat at the head of the table.

Draw a long rectangle on a piece of paper and write "Loving, Wise Self" at the head, and fill in the rest of the seats with the supporting cast members of your inner world, the parts that make a lot of noise: Fear, Loneliness, Judgment, Arrogance, and the like. When you engage with any of these parts, you do so with the resolute commitment to keep your parent at the head of the conversation. We make room for Judgment, but we don't let it run the show. We explore the churning waters of Fear while the parent holds the tether on solid shore.

On one level, anxiety is your young self hanging alone on the clothesline to dry. As soon as you show up with a loving inner parent, even just by doing the exercise in this chapter, anxiety is reduced a notch or two. The more you grow this solid, grounded part of you, the less anxious you will feel.

8

THE REALM OF THE BODY

> This is your body, your greatest gift, pregnant
> with wisdom you do not hear, grief you thought
> was forgotten, and joy you have never known.
>
> MARION WOODMAN
> *Coming Home to Myself: Reflections for*
> *Nurturing a Woman's Body and Soul*

Our bodies are the vessels through which we receive messages and information, the temple by which we know ourselves. Like any temple, the greater respect we show for it, the more holy, and the more known, the space becomes. If our bodies are clogged with sugar, alcohol, and processed foods, if we're not getting enough exercise or sleep, if our hormones are out of balance, the chambers in the temple become difficult to access. Conversely, when we learn to attend to our bodies and listen to its messages, we become more clear, and we're more able to access the wisdom that lives in our innermost chambers. Oftentimes, anxiety will communicate to us via the physical realm, and the presence of anxiety is often a message alerting us to the need to take loving care of our physical bodies.

When working with anxiety, I recommend starting from the ground up, which means starting with the body. Our bodies are foundational to wellness, so when anxiety pipes up, it's best to ask, "Is there a basic body need that is asking for my attention?" When my kids are off-kilter in any way, I always inquire about the physical realm first: "Did you get enough sleep last night?" "Have you eaten enough protein today?" "Do you need to run around the block a few times?" "Have you eaten too much sugar?" I apply the same line of questioning to myself, with the addition of a question centered around hormones.

The Physical Symptoms of Anxiety

Because we live in a neck-up culture, we tend to ignore our bodies' needs—until they erupt in physical illness or anxiety. In fact, one of psyche's most efficient methods of getting our attention is to present anxiety through the physical body. Of course, sometimes a symptom is just a symptom (as opposed to a manifestation of anxiety), and it's important to rule out any serious physical illness before engaging in the depth mindset that views symptoms as metaphors. For this reason, it can be incredibly calming and helpful to the anxious mind to have a full physical checkup and obtain a clear report before moving forward.

If that last line triggered anxiety, you're not alone. Whenever we're talking about the physical realm, we're in danger of tripping the health anxiety wire that says, "Oh, my goodness. She just said that this particular symptom could really mean there's something wrong with me! I have to see the doctor tomorrow!" Hold on. Take a deep breath. Now take another one. Try to use this moment as an invitation to access your loving parent/wise self and imagine what you might say to calm the spike. This might sound like, "Yes, it's so scary to think that I might have something seriously wrong with me (validation), but chances are high that I'm fine (reality). I've been here before. Remember when I thought I had [reference a historical situation where you called anxiety's bluff]? It turned out I was fine. If I'm due for a full medical physical, then I will schedule that, but let's keep reading and become curious about what else these physical manifestations of anxiety might be pointing to (curiosity)."

As I shared in chapter 1, it can be highly calming for the anxious mind to read a list of how anxiety can commonly manifest physically, so that the next time your throat closes or you feel hot and sweaty, you can say, "This is anxiety," instead of allowing fear to run off with the baton of a new catastrophic story. Let's review a more in-depth list of the physical symptoms of anxiety.

Common physical manifestations of anxiety include:

- tightness in chest
- feeling like throat is closing
- difficulty breathing
- difficulty swallowing
- pit in stomach
- lack of appetite
- insomnia
- body shakes, trembling, and chills
- burning or itching skin
- chest pains
- exhaustion
- feeling cold or freezing
- feeling sick
- feeling wrong, weird, odd
- frequent urination
- heart palpitations
- racing heart
- motion sickness
- muscle twitching
- nausea
- headaches
- head pain
- tension in forehead
- difficulty speaking
- shortness of breath—like you can't get a full breath
- feeling of unreality
- stomachache
- digestive disorders
- diarrhea
- tightness in rib cage

Many of these symptoms can be manifestations of emotional needs *and* caused by aspects of your physical health that need attention. The most common areas of the physical realm that I see in my work that can cause and exacerbate anxiety are around blood sugar, food, alcohol, exercise, sleep, and hormones. For many people, anxiety can be a wake-up call to attend to these critical areas of self. Some basic reminders regarding these areas can help you as your loving parent steps up to the plate and decides what new, healthy habits might help create less anxiety and more well-being, mental clarity, energy, and equanimity.

Low Blood Sugar and Anxiety

We need a consistent balance of protein, carbohydrates, fiber, and minerals to experience optimal health. We also need to limit our intake of stimulants, especially if we're highly sensitive people. By stimulants, I mean sugar, caffeine, alcohol, and drugs. What this looks like on a daily basis is some version of the following.

- Eat a high-protein, low/no sugar meal with some carbohydrates within one hour of waking up.

- Eat a high-protein snack every two hours.

- Snack on vegetables as much as you want and enjoy some fruit.

- Eat a high-protein, low/no sugar meal with some carbohydrates three times a day.

- If you struggle with maintaining stable blood-sugar levels, you may need to eat a snack before you go to sleep.

When blood sugar drops, it takes until the next morning for your body to reset. That's why it's so important to keep your blood sugar stable throughout the day by eating shortly after waking up and eating regularly throughout the day.

Symptoms of low blood sugar include (from everydayhealth.com):

- **Anxiety.** "When glucose levels fall too low, your body tells the adrenal glands to release the hormone epinephrine (also called adrenaline), which signals the liver to make more sugar. The excess epinephrine creates an 'adrenaline rush,' which can make you feel anxious."

- **Restless nights.** "Nocturnal hypoglycemia, which is very common, can cause a number of sleep disturbances. Symptoms include night sweats, nightmares, episodes of waking suddenly and crying out, and feelings of unrest and confusion upon waking. A snack before bed can reduce the frequency and severity of sleep disturbances."

- **Emotional instability.** "Mood swings and sudden emotional episodes not typical of your normal behavior are among the neurological symptoms of hypoglycemia, including irrational outbursts, random or hysterical crying, uncontrollable anger, and a strong desire to be left alone. Mild mood changes that may not be as severe, such as general irritability or becoming easily annoyed, can also be a signal that your blood sugar may be dropping." You may also notice that the feeling of nameless dread and intrusive thoughts become more pronounced when blood sugar drops.

Given these immediate changes to your body when your blood sugar is off, you can understand why I recommend looking at the physical realm first when you want to address your anxiety. Trying to journal or meditate when your blood sugar has dropped is like trying to get a car to run by fixing the engine instead of checking the gas tank first. Your blood sugar is the fuel in your gas tank, and if you're on the anxious spectrum, it would behoove you to keep it full.

Food and Anxiety

Many people notice a strong connection between what they're ingesting and their anxiety levels. Just as parents must responsibly decide what goes into their kids' bodies, so you, as the parent of your body, must decide what makes you feel good, clear, connected, alive, and loved and, conversely, what makes you feel anxious. Paying attention to what you ingest means asking yourself, "What makes me feel good in the long run? What helps me feel clear and alive, and what makes me feel irritable, anxious, and shut down?"

Ask yourself and begin to notice how you feel when you eat, drink, or ingest:

- sugar
- caffeine
- alcohol
- nicotine
- marijuana
- chips
- soft drinks
- dairy
- grains

Ingesting stimulating substances will amplify your anxiety by amping up your nervous system. While caffeine and sugar don't have a negative effect on everyone, I've found with the vast majority of my clients that when they reduce or eliminate these substances from their diet, their anxiety lessens and they find themselves more available to connect with themselves and those around them.

It requires discipline to remove certain foods from your diet, but it's part of learning to be a loving parent to your body as you say, "I know you would like to eat cookies every day, but I can see that they're causing you to feel anxious or irritable, so we're going to have to take a break from them." Everyone has their own tolerance levels for toxins or allergens, so it's important that you stay connected to your body and notice the effect that different foods have on your emotional state.

There are no blanket rules when it comes to food; there's only your particular relationship to food and your body.

Note: It's also easy for me to say, "Take a break," but if food/drugs/substances have become a replacement for true nourishment (connecting inside) or a way to escape your uncomfortable feelings, then it's no longer on the level of simply deciding to cut it out but has become more of an addiction. The work then is deeper and longer and requires consistently committing to tuning inside so that you stop abandoning yourself and learn about what it means to love yourself on all levels. This isn't something that will happen quickly, but perhaps another seed will be planted that will inspire to you to take more loving actions on your own behalf.

Alcohol and Anxiety

"I had so much anxiety this weekend," a client will share with me during a Monday session. "I had been feeling so good for the past couple of weeks, but this weekend, I seemed to have taken five giant steps backward."

"Tell me about your weekend," I'll say.

"Well, my boyfriend and I went out with some friends on Friday night, and I had a couple of drinks. Then we went to a wedding on Saturday and drank a bit too much. I woke up Sunday morning feeling pretty crappy. And I spent the rest of Sunday with the familiar pit of anxiety in my stomach. All my familiar mental obsessions and ruminations came barreling into my brain: What if I don't love my boyfriend enough? What if I'm gay? You know how it goes."

"Yes, I do. Any idea what triggered it?" I'll ask, although I already know the answer.

"Probably the alcohol."

"Yes, probably."

It's astonishing to me how many times I've had this conversation with countless clients. And the solution seems simple: if alcohol is scientifically known to stir up anxiety, then eliminating or significantly reducing its consumption would reduce anxiety. Yet when I offer this suggestion, I'm often met with resistance. It's not like when I suggest reducing or eliminating sugar, gluten, or grains. Those aren't easy to eliminate, but they don't occupy the same social status in our culture that alcohol does.

We live in an alcohol-addicted culture. Alcohol is used as a social lubricant and has become such a crutch for most people to feel comfortable socially that they feel lost without it. The paradox is that while alcohol serves as a social lubricant and works in the moment to stave off anxiety, the aftermath of alcohol consumption, especially for highly sensitive people, is an anxiety hangover that often lasts several days. Is it worth it to sacrifice your mental well-being for a couple of drinks?

Many of my clients share that they feel better when they eliminate alcohol completely from their lives. "I really shouldn't have one single sip," they say. Others feel fine with modified use of alcohol, meaning a half a glass of wine every few weeks. But in order to make these changes they first have to get past their resistance.

Some of the resistance has its roots in the fact that they've always struggled socially and have self-diagnosed as having social anxiety. When I hear this self-diagnosis, I'll ask the following questions: "Do you struggle when you're hanging out in a small group of people or just in large gatherings?" *Just in large gatherings.* "Do you struggle socially when you're with a group where there is a common interest, and partying isn't the focus?" *No.* "What's your favorite way to socialize: with a small group, or one-on-one?" *One-on-one.*

Then I'll offer my new "diagnosis": You don't have social anxiety; you're an introvert.

When you know yourself and know where you thrive, you can stop trying to squeeze yourself into the culturally prescribed model for "cool" and "fun." Clients will often share with me that when they stop drinking and partying on the weekends, their friends or roommates will poke fun at them for being boring. "So what?" they respond. "I'm not bored with my life. I'm happy, and I'm living without anxiety."

It requires courage to step outside the box. There can be no doubt that we live in an extroverted, drinking culture. When you step out of that model, you're stepping out of the mainstream. But in making the choice to party less or not at all—which greatly supports your decision to reduce alcohol consumption—you're making a very loving choice for yourself, one that not only honors your wiring, but one that places your desire for an anxiety-free life above your desire to fit in.

Exercise

When it comes to anxiety, exercise is both prophylactic and prescriptive: when we exercise regularly, we create a less inviting environment in our physical body for anxiety to take hold; *and* when anxiety is stirring, exercise reduces its intensity. Exercise is literally medicine in that it releases endorphins as well as the neurotransmitter norepinephrine, both of which improve mental clarity, the ability to handle stress, self-esteem, and sleep. The Anxiety and Depression Association of America says that "a brisk walk or other simple activity can deliver several hours of relief, similar to taking an aspirin for a headache." And a study from the Harvard Medical School Special Health Report showed that exercise can be as effective as antidepressant medication, and its effects last longer.

Human bodies are designed to move throughout the day, yet we've become an increasingly sedentary and lazy culture. For most of human history, in fact, people have moved their bodies as part of their daily lives. Like wild animals, people exercising wasn't something separate from the rhythm of life any more than eating. In other words, people didn't intentionally exercise so much as the way they lived their lives—hunting, cooking, washing, walking down to the water—kept their bodies fit and healthy. Because modern work is largely sedentary, we now have to make a point of moving our bodies on a daily basis. What we've gained in modern conveniences we've lost in terms of an effortless relationship to physical health. If you live a highly sedentary life, one of anxiety's messages is to get up and move.

Many people struggle to find a form of exercise that they can commit to consistently. They also become overwhelmed by the belief that exercise has to come in a certain package or look a certain way. We need to move our bodies, but that doesn't mean we need to join the gym and suffer through an aerobics class five times a week (unless that's your thing). In fact, according to the Anxiety and Depression Association of America, "Psychologists studying how exercise relieves anxiety and depression suggest that a 10-minute walk may be just as good as a 45-minute workout."

Without a doubt, most of us have to make an effort if we're going to move our bodies regularly. But you're not going to exercise if you don't enjoy it. If exercise feels only like drudgery, it's going to fall to the bottom of your list of priorities, and resistance will win every time the subject arises. To circumvent resistance, it's important to start small with activities that you truly enjoy. Usually this includes something that has a secondary gain, like walking while talking to a friend or gardening while enjoying the peacefulness of being outside. If you're not already doing so, try to find a way to exercise that feels nourishing and enjoyable for you.

Sleep

When it comes to anxiety, sleep is a tricky topic to discuss. While you know that getting enough sleep is healthy on many levels and can reduce anxiety, if sleep is already a source of anxiety for you because you struggle with insomnia, then hearing about how essential it is will only create more anxiety. And since anxiety and insomnia go hand in hand—sixty million people are diagnosed with sleep disorders each year in this country—it's quite likely that if you're reading this book, you've suffered or are currently suffering from insomnia.

What I will say is this: if you're not getting enough sleep and *it's because of choices that you're making*—staying up too late playing video games or watching YouTube videos—consider making a change in those areas. Just like a loving parent makes sure that their child develops healthy sleep habits and encourages them to go to bed at a reasonable hour, so one of the jobs of our inner parent is to say, "I know you want to watch one more episode, but it's time to go to bed." If you're hooked on a show, for example, it can take a concerted effort to extricate yourself from the magnetic pull of the screen. If you can remind yourself that it's not worth it because being tired the next day will amplify your anxiety, you'll have a better chance at making the loving choice.

However, if you're not getting enough sleep because you try to go to bed on time, but you suffer from insomnia, keep reading. Insomnia has many causes, all of which are messengers about one or several areas of self—body, heart, mind, or soul—that need attention. Insomnia might be telling you that you need more exercise or that you need to learn how to regulate your blood sugar. It might be telling you that you're not spending enough quiet time nourishing your soul during the day, so it wakes you up so you can absorb the stillness of night. Insomnia is one of anxiety's most powerful emissaries since it's easy to avoid anxiety's call during the busyness and noisiness of daytime life, but it's a lot harder to ignore it in the silence and dark of night. The more you address your anxiety from the root and listen to the messages that are knocking on the door of your psyche at 3:00 a.m., the more health you will find with sleep.

Hormones

There is wisdom in hormones just as there is in anxiety, for they are messengers alerting you not only to physical imbalances, but also to areas in the realms of your emotions and soul that need attention. We live with a rampant cultural brainwashing that seeks to denigrate women and invalidate their experience during times of the month and their lives when hormones are particularly loud, most often around their period and during menopause. We have even named the week before a woman's period as a syndrome and colloquially refer to it as PMS. Any emotions or needs a woman expresses during times of heightened hormones are often invalidated, both by herself and others around her, with the dismissive statement of "It's just hormones." There is the corresponding belief that hormones make women crazy and irrational. The truth is that these are times when women are stripped of certain hormones that normally create a buffer, so we're given an opportunity to see more clearly mindsets and patterns of behavior that aren't serving us. We aren't irrational or crazy; we're simply seeing what has been veiled over the rest of the month or in the decades leading up to menopause. The challenge is to learn to speak our needs clearly and kindly, but the content of what we're seeing shouldn't be invalidated by the sweeping statement of "It's just hormones."

By the way, if that last paragraph triggered anxiety because your fear-based thoughts are more intense during these times and you're wondering now if you're supposed to heed them as truth, call on your loving inner parent to remind you that the anxiety stories aren't your truth but distress flares pointing to places inside that are off-kilter and need attention. If you take the thoughts at face value, you'll fall down the rabbit hole of anxiety, but if you see them as louder messengers during these hormonal seasons of your life, you will begin to hear the deeper messages. (More on working with these thoughts in the next chapter.)

There's no question that a hormonal imbalance can wreak havoc on well-being; hormones can cause anxiety, and anxiety in turn can exacerbate hormones. In other words, sometimes anxiety's message is that there's a hormonal imbalance that needs attention, while other times, when you can attend to other aspects of your four realms of self, your hormones rebalance. If you're seeking to balance your hormones, I encourage you to be careful about how you address them. The medical culture seeks to eradicate the uncomfortable symptoms known as premenstrual syndrome, or PMS, by prescribing medication, usually the birth control pill. What is not addressed is that not only will the pill fail to address the root causes of the hormonal imbalance, but the medication itself can also cause immense anxiety. If the onset or increase of your anxiety correlated to starting the pill, as it has for many of my clients, I encourage you to consider other methods for addressing your hormonal imbalance. The most effective way is working with a skilled naturopath. If that's not feasible for you, there are many books on alternative healing that can help you achieve more balance.

As with anxiety, when you shift from trying to get rid of the discomfort of hormones to learning to meet it, you will begin to decipher the messages. One of the most common messages that arises during these times of shifting hormones is the need to withdraw from the hubbub of life and turn inward where you can hear yourself and be with yourself. If you're a man reading this, keep in mind that men experience hormonal shifts as well. People toss around funny phrases like "He-MS" and "manopause," but there is truth in these jokes. There is no doubt that there are times in men's lives when physiological changes invite emotional and psychological shifts. For both men and women, when we don't listen to the messages embedded in hormonal changes, anxiety increases. But when we shift our mindset and see hormonal communications as another messenger from the body, inviting us toward consciousness, we begin to hear the messages, and anxiety quiets down.

PRACTICE A THIRTY-DAY CHALLENGE

If you haven't reduced or eliminated sugar, caffeine, or alcohol from your diet, begin to notice any relationship between these stimulants and your anxiety. If you've already done that, I encourage you to commit to one change in the physical realm for thirty days that you intuitively sense would help you feel calmer and clearer. This could be eating a healthy, low-sugar, high-protein breakfast every day. It could be making sure that you're in bed by 10:00 p.m. (without outside distraction). It could be taking a short, brisk walk every day. Commit to a simple and doable change, and actively notice and record any positive effects it has on your anxiety.

9

THE REALM OF THOUGHTS

The mind is where the soul goes to hide from the heart.

MICHAEL SINGER

Moving on through the four realms of self, we shift from body to mind as we learn about how to meet our thoughts, discern the difference between truth and falsehood, correct cognitive distortions, and respond to our thoughts from a place of clarity and wisdom. Growing up, we learn math and reading, history and geography, but nobody teaches us about the logic of the mind and how to navigate the internal geography of our mental landscape. A significant aspect of anxiety arises when we don't understand how to work with the normal and necessary thoughts that dart and dash through the mind every minute of every day. The most painful and alarming of these thoughts, the ones that can cascade into anxiety and panic and cause untold mental suffering, are what we call intrusive thoughts.

Intrusive Thoughts and the Cognitive Manifestations of Anxiety

Just as anxiety can manifest in the body, so it can manifest in the mind in the form of thoughts and obsessions. I've never met someone on the anxious spectrum who hasn't suffered from intrusive thoughts at some point in their life (usually starting in childhood or adolescence). For example, our culture emphasizes the phrase "doubt means don't." So when we find ourselves with intrusive thoughts like "Am I with the wrong partner? or "Am I in the wrong career?" we think it must be true. There's no faster way to send the anxious mind into obsessive, self-hatred overdrive than to confirm that an intrusive thought is categorically true.

What exactly is an intrusive thought? An intrusive thought is a repetitive, unwanted, and pervasive thought that causes suffering and prevents you from being present for your life.

We all have thousands of thoughts that enter our minds all day long. But unlike most of them, an intrusive thought sends its talons into consciousness and doesn't let go. It convinces you that it's true and causes inner torment. Let's review the most common intrusive thoughts I come across. Even if your specific thought isn't listed here, believe me when I tell you that there isn't an intrusive thought on the planet that would surprise me:

- What if I'm with the wrong partner?
- What if I don't love my partner enough?
- What if I don't love my child?
- What if I'm straight?
- What if I'm gay?
- What if I'm in the wrong city?
- What if there's a better house for me?
- What if I'm in the wrong job/career?
- What if I've missed my calling?
- What if I was sexually molested, and I don't remember?
- What if I was unfaithful?
- What if I don't have enough friends?
- What if I hurt someone?
- What if I hurt a child?
- What if there's a terrorist attack?
- What if the world ends?
- What if I kill someone?
- What if the plane crashes?
- What if my child gets hurt in some way
  (kidnapped, abused, killed)?

- What if I have an STD?
- What if I have a terminal illness?
- What if I never get pregnant?
- What if there's something wrong with my unborn child?
- What if I do something embarrassing in public?
- What if I end up homeless and alone?
- What if I lose all my money?
- What if I die in my sleep?
- For young children the most common intrusive thought is: What if my parents die? For early to midteens the most common intrusive thought is: What if I'm gay?

And don't let the ego—which wants to tear down any theory that undermines its growth-defying tactics—try to convince you that because your thoughts don't start with the words "what if" but are presented as statements or facts, they're not intrusive thoughts but true thoughts. That's the ego-mind's oldest trick in the book. Following are some other truths about intrusive thoughts.

- Suffering from intrusive thoughts is a mental addiction. It's not a substance addiction (drugs, alcohol, coffee, food) and it's not a process addiction (porn, gaming, screens, shopping), but it functions in a similar way in that it serves to anesthetize emotional pain and protect you from being fully present.

- Intrusive thoughts are brilliant defense mechanisms in that they protect you from accessing more vulnerable feelings.

- Intrusive thoughts often point toward perfection. They whisper in your ear a story that carries as its subtext the belief that if you could attain the perfect partner, job, house, or child, you will be lifted out of the suffering of being human.

As I mentioned, one of the defining qualities of an intrusive thought is that it appears as truth. For the untrained mind, it can be difficult to distinguish between the thoughts and the truth, and this is often a starting point for anxiety: if you believe that the thoughts are true, you hook into them and get stuck on spin cycle. Shifting from an untrained mind to a trained mind is one of the keys to healing from anxiety. Two of the defining attributes of the trained mind are the ability to decide which thoughts need attention and to discern between truth and hook. In order to do this, you must first develop the skill of noticing then accessing the choice-point: that moment between stimulus (the thought) and response (how you respond to the thought).

Accessing the Choice-Point

Some of the most common statements I say to clients and course members about thoughts are:

- Just because you think it doesn't mean it's true.

- Everyone has dark, weird, unusual, silly, and crazy thoughts, but very few people talk about them. Having dark thoughts doesn't make you a bad person.

- A vast canyon lies between thoughts and actions.

Somewhere along the way, we learned to bow down to every thought and feeling that crosses into consciousness. Or maybe it's more accurate to say that we never learned to cultivate the muscle of discernment that allows us to determine which thoughts are true and which are false. Furthermore, and perhaps even more detrimental, is that because we live in a buttoned-up culture that presents only a happy face, we have no way of knowing that every human has dark thoughts from time to time. In the absence of normalization, shame takes root and sprouts, and we already know that it's a short step from shame to anxiety. Shame and curiosity are mutually exclusive: when you remove the shame with the awareness that all of your thoughts are normal and common, you will be able to address them more effectively and with more curiosity.

Once normalized, accessing the choice-point is key; otherwise you become a victim of your thoughts. A thought enters your mind like "I'm in the wrong city" or "I have cancer," and you immediately latch onto it as the truth. The next thing you know, you're spinning into a tizzy of anxiety, caught up in the magnetic energy of the thought you believed to be truth. Or you cringe when your wife comes over to you for a hug and a kiss; you fall prey to the power of the fear/resistance and a story line that assigns meaning to your response, which causes you to constrict and turn away from her ever so subtly.

This is why developing a strong, wise presence inside of you (inner parent/wise self) that can make choices based on clear intellect and values rather than fleeting thoughts and feelings is essential. Without this strength of inner self, you will be buffeted around by the thoughts and feelings that fluctuate like hormones inside your mind and body. If you're navigating your life by the compass of thoughts and feelings, you will live on a stormy sea, indeed. It would be like allowing your three-year-old to run your household.

What are the alternatives? When you have access to the choice-point—the pause between a thought or feeling and believing it or acting on it—you win back all your power. Viktor Frankl is credited with saying, *"Between stimulus and response there is a space. In that space is our power to choose our response. In our response lies our growth and our freedom."* It's in that small yet decisive moment between thought and action that you can say, "Do I want to latch on to this thought?" If you could slow life down to micromoments, if you could alter time like a movie, turning it into slow motion and elongating the critical moment when your mind veers off like a runaway locomotive and instead redirect it to stay on the smooth track of clear thinking, everything would change. As challenging as it sounds, that's exactly what you must do if you're going to rewire the brain to respond to the stimulus in a different way so that you don't send the anxious mind into overdrive.

Let's take the example of the man who hooks into the resistance and pushes his wife away. The man could think, "This feeling in my body means I don't really love her," thereby perpetuating the feeling, which quite likely originates in a fear-based place inside of him. If he believes that thought-story, his fear-wall will become fortified. If, on the other hand, he names the thought as a story and decides to challenge it or brush it aside, he's taken one critical step toward unhooking from an anxious spiral. He can then choose his next action, which, without the lie in the way, will hopefully be a bit of softness toward his wife.

It's the story he's telling himself in that moment that determines what happens next and next and next. His freedom lies in that crucial moment between the stimulus and response. This is true anytime an anxiety story takes hold: the sooner you can recognize it as an intrusive or fear-based thought, the faster you can regain control and avoid slipping down the rabbit hole of anxiety.

Developing Discernment: Whatever You Water Will Grow

Once the choice-point is accessed, the loving inner parent who executes clear decisions and sets boundaries can decide which thoughts to explore, how to explore them, and which ones to brush aside. In other words, you want to accept the thought instead of shoving it behind a web of shame, but you don't want to give it too much attention. Until they learn to work effectively with thoughts, most people tend to vacillate between two polarities: on the one hand, they avoid the thought and try to shut it down with shame, and on the other, they indulge the thought by seeking reassurance, Googling, and talking about it, and then discovering that thoughts feed on attention. The more you feed a negative thought, the bigger it gets, until it takes over your mind completely.

Whatever we water will grow.

This concept was illuminated for me one summer many years ago when I was determined to grow a beautiful, thriving garden. In spring, I packed away my excuses—not enough time; it's impossible with a toddler underfoot—and proceeded, under the tutelage of my dear friend, to begin my seedlings in greenhouses beneath homemade lightboxes. My older son and I attended to the plantings faithfully each day and delighted as each little green sprout poked its head above ground. We watered them, transplanted them, and loved them. (Everest insisted on eating lunch beside them to make sure they felt loved.) And when it was finally time to transplant them outdoors, we did so with tender loving care. This would surely be the year when we picked peas and kale straight from our own backyard!

All proceeded well for several weeks. I found time to water and weed each day and, sure enough, the peas began to flourish. My soul soared as my son and I picked sweet peas every day and munched on them during my baby's naps. Amid the fullness of my life, the fifteen minutes a day that I carved out to devote to the garden became a ritual that nourished me with pure joy. Nothing made me happier than walking down to the creek to fill up two watering cans, then slowly watering around the base of each plant.

And then the rains came. It rained torrents every day for weeks, and when I returned to my garden after a few days of absence, I never expected the sight that lay before me: a riot of weeds. Weeds tangling around the peas. Weeds threatening to choke the kale and cucumbers. Weeds cavorting with the beans. Weeds laughing in the pumpkin patch. My precise hand-watering had been overtaken by a few days of nature's indiscriminate watering system.

You might be wondering what this has to do with thoughts and the healing process. I'll tell you: When a negative thought pops into your head, you have a choice regarding how you want to respond to that thought. If you water it, it will grow, just like the unwanted weeds in my garden. The longer you water the thought, the bigger it will grow. And once the negative thought has grown to the size of a roadside California weed, you have to work very hard to dig it out by the roots. You have to get down on your hands and knees and pull. And if that doesn't work, you get out the trowel or pitchfork and dig until the root breaks. It's so much easier to nip the thought in the bud by learning how to work with it effectively, which in many cases means not giving it any water.

Each thought is a seed. You can't control which seeds land in the garden of your mind; they arrive on the winds of life without permission or warning. For example, you could be happily spending the morning with your newborn baby when the thought arises, "What if I suddenly hurt him?" At that moment, you have a choice. You can water the thought with more fear-based thoughts like, "Oh, my goodness. I've had the thought that I'm going to hurt my baby. That must mean that deep down I don't really love him. What if something takes over me and I harm him? What if I can't control myself?" Then you're off and running in a tizzy of new-mother anxiety. Or you can rein in the habitual fear response, access a rational part of your mind, and say, "Most new mothers have that thought at some point. I'm exhausted and overwhelmed, and I know I love my baby. I'm not going to pay this thought a moment's more attention right now, but when I have some time, I will ask what the thought may be pointing to inside of me that needs attention."

Similarly, I've worked with many new mothers who, while madly in love with their babies, have the thought "I hate you" pop into their heads. When we unpack the thought, what we find every time is that "I hate you" is a placeholder for "I hate *this*: I hate being so exhausted, overwhelmed, not knowing what I'm doing, alone." Quite frequently, thoughts are not what they seem, and when we have access to the choice-point, we can decide which thoughts to brush aside and which are arrows and metaphors pointing to other messages or deeper needs.

PRACTICE IDENTIFY HOW YOU WATER YOUR THOUGHTS

Take a few minutes to identify which of the following ways you water your thoughts.

- Talking about the thoughts, or seeking reassurance

- Journaling about the thoughts (Journaling can be a powerful tool if used correctly, but if you're

journaling about the thoughts themselves, or
any sneaky subsets of the primary thoughts,
you will remain trapped in the thought.)

- Googling

- Thinking/ruminating/obsessing

- Researching

Now reflect on how you feel when you indulge in
these reassurance-seeking tactics. Does your anxiety
momentarily subside? Does it make your anxiety worse?
Now pause and imagine—literally see yourself—*not*
indulging in these tactics and instead simply observing the
thought and asking yourself how you want to respond.

Symbols, Metaphors, and Dreams

Another key to working with thoughts and accessing the critical choice-
point is learning how not to take every thought literally. One of the many
problems of living in an image-based, superficial culture is that you learn
to take *everything* at face value. You have a dream about having sex with
someone other than your partner, and you latch on to the most obvious
interpretation: you secretly want to have sex with someone else. Then you
begin having anxiety about your marriage. You find yourself obsessively
thinking about your ex, and you assume it means you still want to be
with him or her, which leads to relationship anxiety. You bolt awake in
the middle of the night from a nightmare that you have cancer, and you
believe that you have cancer (despite the fact that you just received a clean
bill of health at your last physical). Now you're on the road to health
anxiety. Your child screams at you, and you assume that he's trying to
control you or needs a lesson in manners and respect. These seem like
reasonable enough interpretations, and they're certainly supported by the
mainstream culture, but there are other meanings at play.

By contrast, part of the reason that people respond to my work with a breath of relief is that I take very little at face value. True to the Jungian perspective, in which I've been trained, I understand sex dreams as symbols that you're longing to unite with an underdeveloped part of you that the dream figure represents. I understand intrusive thoughts about an ex as an indicator that you're needing closure with that person or that a part of you is represented by that person. I understand death dreams, especially in the form of nightmares, as metaphors that usually mean a part of us is ready to "die," and a new part is ready to be born. And I understand the relentless screams of a five-year-old as a symptom that a primary need isn't being met, and that he's communicating this unmet need in the only way he knows how. These are just one possible interpretation of dreams, intrusive thoughts, doubt, and difficult behavior in kids. My point is that we should not interpret life by what we see on the surface. In fact, neuroscience has now proven what depth psychologists and mystics have intuited for centuries: the conscious mind runs the show, at best, only about 5 percent of the time (to paraphrase Bruce Lipton).

The gift that Sigmund Freud and Carl Jung brought to modern psychology is the awareness of the unconscious, which is everything that exists below conscious awareness. Feelings are not always what we think they are. Longings point to worlds upon worlds of inner needs. When we learn to interpret symptoms as metaphors that stand for deeper needs and longings, the kaleidoscopic, multidimensional, timeless world of the unconscious opens up to us. We become adept at digging deep and, ultimately, at taking full responsibility for our inner realms. Life becomes less simplistic but a lot more interesting and, perhaps paradoxically, less scary. For when we're tapped into the underground river of the unconscious instead of living on the surface, we're living life from the place of essence instead of image. We're connected to what's true and sustainable instead of what's fleeting and ephemeral. We anchor into the collective unconscious of generations past and the invisible web that connects humanity. These moves that join us to essence, the ephemeral world, and the invisible strands of connection are some of the most powerful antidotes to anxiety. For this reason, the shift in mindset from the literal to the metaphoric is another key to transformation.

Because we've been conditioned since birth to think literally and take thoughts and physical symptoms at face value, it takes time to train our brains to think in terms of metaphor. But when we remember that the body speaks in metaphor and the unconscious loves to play on words in dreams and in symptoms, our minds awaken and anxiety dissipates. As I've been steeped in the world of the unconscious my entire life, this way of thinking is second nature for me. When a client says, "No matter how much I eat before bed, I'm always hungry," I think, "What are you hungry for—nurturing, comfort, forgiveness?" A client says, "I've been having heartburn the last two weeks," and I wonder, "What is burning in your heart?" A client says, "I had a dream that I died," and I muse, "What part of you has died, and what new part is ready to be reborn?"

It's not always appropriate to share these musings, but when I do and they hit home, there's almost always an immediate eruption of a smile that indicates an aha moment, the kind that bypasses the mind and hits at the level of body. These moments indicate that we've hit on truth and are making inroads to healing. Anxiety has done its job; the unconscious has been made conscious, and the ball of healing is set in motion.

PRACTICE
AN EXERCISE IN METAPHORS

Write down your top five anxiety-based thoughts, feelings, and physical symptoms, and open your mind to imagine what the metaphor might be. Notice how it feels when you think in terms of metaphor as opposed to taking the thoughts at face value.

The Metaphor of Intrusive Thoughts

Thoughts require different kinds of attention depending on their frequency and their message. Sometimes a dark or strange thought enters your mind, and you can brush it aside with a quick, normalizing statement (like the earlier example of the mother and her baby). If you do this enough times, *and the thought isn't an emissary for anxiety designed to bring a message through the metaphor of an intrusive thought*, the thought will wither and die.

However, quite often, intrusive thoughts are indeed messengers bearing tremendous gifts, and the work is to see the thought as a metaphor, then unpack it to arrive at the gem at the center. In all of my courses, I teach the tool of using a wheel to decipher a thought: drawing a circle at the center of a piece of paper, writing the thought in the middle, then drawing several lines coming out of it like the rays of the sun. At the end of each line, you'll write the real wound, feeling, or belief that needs attention—what the intrusive thought is pointing to.

For example, one of the most common intrusive thoughts that lands people at my virtual doorstep is, "I'm not attracted enough to my partner." Taken literally (especially in our image-based culture, which places irresistible physical attraction at the top of the nonnegotiable qualities-I-must-have-in-a-partner list), most people's response to that thought would be, "Then you should leave." However, having worked with thousands of people who have been able to move beyond the habitual response of reading the thought at face value and have instead found the courage to hear it as a messenger—and remained in their healthy, loving relationships—I know that this thought is a metaphor. Figure 2, Not-Attracted-to-Partner Wheel, comes from a client who was hit full-force with the attraction spike during her third trimester of pregnancy. It represents what breaking this thought apart looks like and decodes its messages.

Keep in mind that these wheels will look different for everyone. For many people, the metaphor embedded inside of "I'm not attracted to you" is "I'm not attracted to *me*" or "I'm not attracted to *life*." Both could point to old or current wounds around adequacy and self-worth or areas in life where you've lost juice. When you can train yourself

Spiritual/Creative/Well of Self

- It's early spring: recognizing that, as a highly sensitive person, I'm always attuned to the seasonal shifts.

- General lack of connection to my creativity; realizing that as a child I was always making things and I don't do that anymore.

- Knowing that there is something bigger for my life and not moving toward that.

Cognitive

- Habit of attaching to thoughts as truth
- Quick douse of truth-water:
- I'm not attracted to my partner = I'm making my partner responsible for my aliveness.

Intrusive Thought: I'm Not Attracted

Emotional

- What am I avoiding feeling?
- Recently moved—needs to grieve the transition but hasn't had time alone
- Staying with family: seeing my family with clear eyes—their tendency toward denial
- I am the "seer"
- Addiction and mental illness in the family
- Fears about becoming a mother

Physical

- Thirty weeks pregnant
- Not sleeping well
- Uncomfortable
- Hormonal
- Back hurting

FIGURE 2. NOT-ATTRACTED-TO-PARTNER WHEEL

Need for Certainty

- At the core of intrusive thoughts is the need for certainty, which often derives from the sensitive person's acute awareness of change and death.

- When we can work toward accepting our "fundamental human ambiguity," as Pema Chödrön says, we learn to accept uncertainty and the ego softens into the reality that we have control over very little.

Empty Well of Self

- The intrusive thought is a flare from the inner self calling you to slow down, turn inward, and give time and attention to reflecting on and exploring your inner world.

- Jung said, "What we don't make conscious emerges later as fate."

- When you have a solid adult at the helm you can provide your own solid reassurance.

Untrained Mind

- When you hook into every thought and believe it as truth, you will fall down the rabbit hole of anxiety.

Need for Accurate Information

- This is the cognitive element of intrusive thoughts. Many people don't know the truth about sexuality, anger, high sensitivity, death.

- The thought-flare may need to be doused with truth-water. After that initial douse, the work is to avoid giving the thought further attention through ruminating, reassurance-seeking, or researching (no Google).

The Roots of Intrusive Thoughts

Overload of Emotions

- Many children learn to retreat to the safety of their thoughts and heads in order to manage the big feelings that threaten to overwhelm them with nobody helping them through. It's what Daniel Siegel calls "leaning to the left."

- When we don't attend inward and have spent a lifetime pushing down difficult feelings they have no choice but to boil over and pop out the top in the form of intrusive thoughts.

The Metaphor

- Jung said: We pathologize because we have forgotten how to mythologize.

- We take everything at face value, what Jeremy Taylor calls "mistaken literalism."

- These thoughts are metaphors pointing the way to integration.

FIGURE 3.

UNDERSTANDING THE ROOT CAUSES OF INTRUSIVE THOUGHTS

to see intrusive thoughts as metaphors and strap on your headlight of curiosity, the places that need attention inside your inner world will be revealed.

I'll share another example of a client who was struggling with an intrusive thought about her work for many years. The client had worked in corporate America for fifteen years at a job in which she excelled and that helped her achieve financial success and stability. However, after the birth of her kids, she longed for a change that would give her more autonomy and flexibility. She left her job and quickly established her own business. At first, she thrived, but quite soon she started to notice a niggling doubt: "Is this really my life's work? Is this new job my calling? Shouldn't I be doing something more meaningful? I must be settling." These thoughts sent her on a wild goose chase for many months as she was 100 percent convinced that the thoughts were coming from her "truth." As long as she believed the thoughts, she couldn't challenge them. But believing the thoughts brought her more and more suffering. It was time to break free.

In one defining session, I said to her, "For the fifteen years that you were at your corporate job did you ever have this thought?"

"Not once."

"So here you were at a job that you knew wasn't your calling, yet this intrusive thought that you're settling never came up once."

"That's right."

"What does that tell you?"

"That it's not about my career. It's something that lives inside of me that I would take with me no matter what career I'm in."

"That's right."

"But why didn't it come up in that other job?"

"Because you were focused on relationships at that time. And the job gave you enough stability to quell the ego, which thrives on the illusions of stability, like a consistent paycheck, meeting externally defined goals, getting praise from managers. All the things that corporate life offers."

"Yes. So really I just swapped one intrusive thought for another one. I swapped focusing on relationships for focusing on work."

"That's exactly right. And now it's time to tend to what's embedded inside the intrusive thought. What is needed? What pain are you avoiding by focusing on the thought?"

"My core issues around inadequacy and unworthiness. The need for a definite identity."

"Yes, exactly. And also, I suspect, the need to move toward your fundamental groundlessness."

Intrusive thoughts cover over many core needs and feelings, but at the root is the need for certainty. As our culture fails to guide us to develop an acceptance of the changeable reality that defines our existence, we have a very hard time accepting uncertainty, which is another way of saying that we have a hard time accepting death in all forms. We resist grieving the emotional deaths that occur when we transition to new places in life. We're not guided on how to grieve the pain and loss that punctuate a day. We're not mentored on how to live life fully, which means feeling all our feelings. And when we don't live life fully, we actually fear it, which then creates a fear of death.

Living with Uncertainty: The Call of Intrusive Thoughts

Most mainstream methods of addressing anxiety and intrusive thoughts lead to the Whac-A-Mole game I referred to earlier: once you resolve one question and find enough certainty to move on, if you don't address the root causes of the intrusive thoughts, you'll quickly find yourself trying to bang the mole of a different obsession down the hole. And then you'll find yourself tumbling down into the anxiety rabbit hole, hell-bent on finding the definitive answer to your next soul-shaking question.

It's not that you need to give attention to the thought itself and try to resolve the question. In fact, you can't resolve the question, because these are fundamentally unanswerable questions. There's not a blood test you can take to determine if you're 100 percent straight or gay, if you love your partner "enough," or if you're living in the "right" city. Either you dip down into the place of self-trust and self-knowledge so that you can answer these questions to a satisfactory degree, and/or you start to cultivate a relationship with uncertainty. And that's when you find the gift that lives in the center of intrusive thoughts.

Living with uncertainty. We simply don't like it. We want definitive answers. We want definable goals. We are intrinsically wired to gravitate toward a need for control and a subsequent attempt to create the illusion of control. Our dominant parenting and education models reinforce this basic ego need. When we don't honor the natural rhythm of a child and coerce her into conforming to an externalized model whereby she gains approval, her inborn self-trust is weakened. Adults inadvertently reinforce the ego's need for control instead of helping children cultivate their connection to self, which helps them connect to the transitory flow of life.

The fear-based self believes that if you could answer the intrusive thoughts of the day, you would hedge your bets and *know, without any doubt,* that you're okay. Because the fear-based self is terrified of risk, terrified of anything that touches into vulnerability, it creates elaborate and convincing reasons why you need to change your life or seek certainty in some way. This creates an illusion of control, and as uncomfortable as it is to live in the head-space of anxiety or uncertainty, it's often a preferable state to the ambiguous, vulnerable place of living in your heart. In other words, the question to ask yourself is, "Is it more important for me to remain attached to the illusion of control or to learn about what it means to be loving?" If you want to learn about what it means to be loving to yourself and others, you have to be willing to let go of control.

This obviously doesn't happen in one Hollywood-breakthrough moment of therapeutic enlightenment. Making the choice to learn rather than remain tightly wound in the safe fortress of control *is a daily, sometimes hourly, choice.* It's a terrifying choice, no doubt. It's a choice that flies in the face of every illusion of safety that you've spent a lifetime constructing. It's as terrifying as standing on the cliff of eternity and leaping into the abyss. Let yourself feel that terror. Let yourself begin to befriend the mystery of life instead of clinging to what you think you can control. The truth is that there is so little we can control. We make plans because we want to know what will happen in the next hour, but the unknowable and mysterious force of *life* could subvert your plans in an instant. The only freedom is to make friends with not knowing. When you become more comfortable with the places of not knowing and explore the gifts encased inside the thoughts, the intrusive thoughts will slowly fade away.

PRACTICE FOUR STEPS FOR DISMANTLING INTRUSIVE THOUGHTS

Healing from intrusive thoughts is a multilayered process. Following these basic steps will help you begin to break free from their hold:

1. **Name the thought.** For many people, just naming and normalizing what's happening inside their minds—knowing that the thoughts are not indications that there's something wrong with them but are actually coming in the service of health and healing—is half the battle toward recovery. When you name the thought, you're already de-fusing from it, since naming it requires that you're witnessing it. This one small action is how you begin to widen the gap between stimulus and response.

2. **Expose the lie.** If you believe the thought is true, you will go down the rabbit hole of anxiety and depression. If you can say, "This is my familiar intrusive thought, and even if I think it's true, I know it's not true," you will take an essential step toward de-fusing your attachment to it.

3. **Sit with the underlying feeling.** Once you remove the addiction by naming the thought and exposing

it as a lie, you will be left with what the thought is covering up: a sense of inadequacy, insecurity, vulnerability, sadness, groundlessness of the human experience. Breathe into those feelings and remind yourself that being human—with all of its vulnerability—isn't something that you can get over. It can't be fixed. The best we can do is be with ourselves with love and compassion. And in the loving, we find freedom.

4. **Ask the cut-through question for intrusive thoughts.** "What is this thought protecting me from feeling?" Then be willing to sit in silence until your breath leads you to what is needed, which isn't always an answer as much as a direction, a signpost, a crack of spaciousness in the choke hold of anxiety. Allow your exploration to be led by the headlight of curiosity and cradled in the pillows of compassion. Imagine a warrior strapping on her protective gear and amulets: a shield, a headband with a gem in the middle, a spear. So we, as love-warriors delving into the uncertain inner realms, strap on the gear of our loving inner parent and sit beside the parts of ourselves who are crying out for attention. (You will learn more about how to attend to the feelings inside the intrusive thoughts in the next chapter.)

Once you have a sense of what needs attention, make a wheel. Having a visual representation of the core needs, feelings, and beliefs embedded inside a thought will help you break the habit of immediately attaching to the thought as truth and will help you create a new neural pathway in your brain that learns to view the thoughts as messengers arriving in the guise of metaphor. Use the figures provided earlier in this chapter as guides. 🍃

10

THE REALM OF FEELINGS

> When we block our awareness of feelings, they continue
> to affect us anyway. Research has shown repeatedly
> that even without conscious awareness, neural
> input from the internal world of body and emotion
> influences our reasoning and our decision making. . . .
> In other words, you can run but you cannot hide.
>
> DANIEL J. SIEGEL
> *Mindsight: The New Science of Personal Transformation*

At the center of ourselves, at the very center of our body and our soul, lives the heart. When we allow ourselves to stay in the flow of our feelings—feeling sadness when it reaches out like a child in the dark, feeling jealousy when it pricks the sides of the eyes, feeling anger when it scalds like lava, feeling joy when it hums and laughs—the heart remains open and fully alive, and anxiety is edged to the outer rims.

But more often than not, we plug up our hearts like a cork in a bottle. We do this because we learned early in life, from a culture that doesn't have the faintest clue how to guide its members through big and difficult feelings, to shut down. And when we shut down and cork up the heart enough, the energy system of feelings is often forced to go upward, into the head in the form of thoughts. This is when people often find their way to healing: when the habit of intrusive thoughts has taken hold to such a degree that the person feels imprisoned by their own mind. As Michael Singer writes in *The Untethered Soul*:

If you close around the pain and stop it from passing through, it will stay in you. That is why our natural tendency to resist is so counterproductive. If you don't want the pain, why do you close around it and keep it? Do you actually think that if you resist, it will go away? It's not true. If you release and let the energy pass through, then it will go away. If you relax when the pain comes up inside your heart, and actually dare to face it, it will pass. Every single time you relax and release, a piece of the pain leaves forever. Yet every time you resist and close, you are building up the pain inside. It's like damming up a stream. You are then forced to use the psyche to create a layer of distance between you who experiences the pain and the pain itself. That is what all the noise is inside your mind: an attempt to avoid the stored pain.

Instead of feeling the stored pain, which is raw and vulnerable, we spin up into the safe and familiar refuge of the thought patterns. Instead of dropping down into the body, which is round and amorphous, we become caught in the illusion that if we could only answer this one question, we would find certainty. As such, we continue on in the pattern that began as a defense and protection—retreating to the somewhat safe haven of mind—and continue to avoid our feelings.

Why do we avoid something so natural and essential to healthy living? We avoid it because we've introjected the voices from the culture that have told us from the beginning that our feelings were something to get over, avoid, or ignore, and that there was no place for them at the table of psyche.

As you're reading through the following sections, notice what feelings enter your heart, tighten your chest, ask for release through your throat and mouth. If you can, let the pain emerge: cry, write, dance, breathe. Pain only asks for one thing: to be seen and heard and known. When you move toward it instead of pushing it away, your anxiety will begin to transform as you step into the fullness of being human, which we cannot experience unless we allow ourselves to feel the full spectrum of emotions. Anxiety, once again, is the portal through which we're invited to become more fully ourselves, and a gateway into our more vulnerable feelings. The anxiety grabs our attention, sounds the alarm, and invites us to ask, "What is the anxiety protecting me from feeling?" When we start to thaw out and feel our lives, anxiety, having completed its current mission, fades away.

Anxiety Is a Placeholder for Feelings

One of the strange and fascinating elements about anxiety is that it's not actually a feeling. We feel the manifestations of anxiety in our bodies and minds through physical symptoms and intrusive thoughts, but anxiety itself isn't a real feeling, but instead a placeholder for the vulnerable feelings that we're too scared to feel. I'll elucidate through a story.

One day many years ago, I was out shopping for clothes with my two boys at our favorite consignment store, and my older son said, "Mommy, let's look at some rain boots for Asher."

"Oh, great idea," I responded, and held Asher's hand as we walked to the display. Asher immediately grabbed a pair of ladybug rain boots, an almost identical replica of his big brother's pair that had cracked open to the point of needing to be replaced. Asher tried them on, they were a perfect fit, and we started to walk to the counter when Everest grumbled, "It's not okay that Asher gets new rain boots before I do."

"But you just suggested that we look for new rain boots for him! I don't understand why you're upset," I said, annoyed.

"Because I don't want him to have new boots if I don't have new boots." He grumbled all the way to the cash register.

It was a classic case of sibling envy, but it took me a while to see it.

A few minutes later, as we were driving to our next destination, Everest complained, "It's not okay if Asher wears his boots in the creek before mine arrive."

"It's not okay" was a phrase Everest often said at that time in his life when he was trying to control outer circumstances. I used to try to convince him why it was okay, until I realized that arguing with the fear-and-control-driven ego is pointless. Eventually, I became more adept at first naming his experience, then directing him down into his feelings.

"It sounds like you're trying to control instead of letting yourself feel envious," I said.

"What's envious?" Everest asked.

"It's kind of like jealousy. Jealousy is when you're feeling left out, like when Daddy plays with Asher and makes him laugh really hard. Envy is when you want something that someone else has. They're both really hard feelings to let yourself feel," I explained.

"You mean the green-eyed monster?" Asher piped up. "Humphrey was jealous of Og the Frog." He was referring to one of their favorite book series about Humphrey, the classroom hamster, and how he felt jealous when the teacher brought in a new pet, a frog, and all of the kids went gaga over him.

"Yes, that's jealousy. It's called a monster because it feels so big inside, like it could just swallow you up. Most people try to deny it when they feel jealous or envious, because they think they shouldn't feel that way, but everyone feels those feelings sometimes. They're part of being human.

"But they really are very difficult feelings to feel. A part of you (ego—although I didn't use that term with my kids yet) doesn't believe that you can handle such a big feeling, and it tells you to control other people so that you don't have to feel it. But it doesn't work! You can't control people and circumstances, and it takes a lot of energy to try. In the end, it's much easier to let yourself feel the envy. It's just a feeling—an energy—and it's very uncomfortable, but it will pass through you. When you try to exert control, you become tight inside and the feeling can't get out. Then it becomes trapped inside of you and actually grows bigger. If you can let yourself feel envious, it will pass through you, and eventually you'll arrive at acceptance."

Everest seemed to hear me, and his complaining and controlling quieted down. I could see him visibly exhale. The tightness of control released into acceptance.

I was teaching my kids a simple equation, one that I teach my clients every day:

feel your feelings = acceptance of what is =
flowing with the river of life

VERSUS

avoid the feelings = control what is =
fight the river of life and feel stuck inside

As soon as I identified the feeling encased in the control, the tension broke open for all of us. I stopped trying to convince Everest to focus on something else, and Everest stopped trying to control me and Asher.

We seem wired as humans to try to control outer circumstances in an attempt to avoid painful and uncomfortable feelings. Yet one of the golden keys, one of the ways that we learn to let go and flow in the river of life, is to allow ourselves to feel our feelings. It's a satisfying moment in a session when a client says to me, "I finally understand what you've been saying. Today I noticed my brain swimming and churning and the anxiety building up, and I took a few deep breaths, turned inside, and asked myself, 'What am I feeling right now?' It's usually something like grief or envy or maybe fear of the unknown, and when I just let myself feel it, the anxiety fell away."

Feelings are manageable; anxiety is not. The more you practice cutting through the habit of spider-monkeying up the vines of anxiety that entrap your brain, and instead drop back down into your heart, where your feelings live, the less anxious and more peaceful you will feel.

A Lifetime Habit of Avoiding Pain

It's one thing to say "Just feel your feelings," as if it's as easy as snapping your fingers. Yet when you've spent a lifetime avoiding pain, it takes time, practice, and patience to create new neural pathways that rewire this habit. In order to do this, it's helpful to understand why it's so scary to feel pain. Once you can identify the beliefs that are standing sentry in front of your heart, you can call them out, challenge them, and gently create inroads led by the new message that it's not only safe to feel your pain, but it's also essential for your healing.

There is no doubt that most people will do anything and everything to avoid feeling the basic feelings of life. Some of this is biological, as all species are wired to recoil from pain, both physical and emotional. Some of this is cultural, as Western culture has a particular attraction to the happy face, which means a particular denial of pain and messiness (as discussed in chapter 2). And much of this is because many people still carry a litany of rules, "shoulds," and early memories about their emotional lives, beliefs and patterns absorbed before they even learned to talk.

When you cried as an infant for prolonged periods of time and weren't picked up, something inside shut down. When those undesirable feelings erupted as a child, and you received the literal or metaphoric slap in the face, you were silenced. If you cried alone, which many children will do as the feelings cannot be contained, the only comfort was a thick blanket of shame. Sometimes the cries were so big that it felt like you were going to die. On the heels of these experiences, you may have formed the following beliefs around crying.

- I shouldn't be sad.
- Feelings are weak.
- Crying is shameful.
- If I'm overly emotional, I'm doing something wrong and/or there's something wrong with me.
- Feelings are a waste of time.
- If I let myself cry fully, something bad will happen.
- I feel out of control and too vulnerable when I cry.
- Feelings are an indulgence.
- Crying is for sissies.
- I'm too much, too emotional, too sensitive.
- Crying makes it worse, so what's the point?

It's essential to identify the beliefs you're carrying about pain so that you can assess if they're true or faulty, then decide, with your inner parent at the helm, how to proceed the next time you're aware of pain surfacing.

I often tell my course members the story of teaching my sons to practice Tonglen when we see dead animals on the side of the road. To refresh your memory: the practice is to breathe in what's unwanted—in this case grief, helplessness, heartbreak—and breathe out what's wanted: peace to all beings. The practice teaches us to move toward our pain instead of giving in to the habitual tendency to push it away. For even though my husband and I never shame away emotional reactions to anything in life—and certainly not the true pain of seeing death in any form—our kids still fall prey to the natural response to retreat from pain. In this case, encouraging the practice teaches our kids that every feeling deserves attention. So I'll say something like, "I can see how sad you felt when we passed that dead prairie dog. Let's put our hands on our hearts and breathe into the pain, then breathe out comfort and love to the prairie dog and its family."

When I tell this story, my clients will often say something like, "I would have been shamed if I had expressed pain about roadkill. Even if it wasn't explicit shame, the covert message was to get over it, and that there was something wrong with me for feeling so deeply. I can see how I still give myself this same message: that my pain is too much or too big, which causes me to shame myself, and then I don't make time to listen to it and feel it."

I then talk about guiding our kids through their grief, to which my clients often respond with, "I didn't have anyone to guide me through my grief." Nobody did. We are an emotionally illiterate culture. We focus on facts and left-brained information, on achievement and outcome, and completely ignore the value of feeling our feelings. The guidance isn't difficult, but it would have required having parents who weren't afraid of their own pain, and parents before them who weren't afraid of their pain. And so on, back through the generations, following the ancestral line of well-meaning people who were taught to deny their softest, most vulnerable selves. We, in this generation, are experiencing a rise in emotional consciousness, which allows us to raise more emotionally intelligent kids. And the shift must begin with you and your willingness to soften into your grief places where you can meet your pain with love.

Early and Ancient Pain

There is a room in your heart where sadness dwells. Each story of sadness lives there like a stagnant, frozen particle of light waiting for you to see it, to hold it, to wrap it in a blanket, and bring it tea. When you visit your grief place with love, the particles of light start to shimmer and move—dance, even—for all things, even our pain, especially our pain, want to be seen and loved.

This pain has been with you for a long time. There may be pain from a time before you had words or clear memories: the pain of the newborn being ripped from the womb; the pain of a baby trying to latch on to the breast taken away too early; the pain of a three-year-old being left before she was ready to be left; the pain of not being held when you needed to be held, or being held too much or in the wrong way; the pain of teasing and taunting and bullying; the pain of first love; the pain of a broken heart.

There may likely be sadness in your grief place that is yours but isn't yours: the intergenerational, unlived pain of those who came before you and who didn't bring warm blankets and cups of tea to their grief. Carl Jung wrote that we live the unlived lives of our parents and grandparents, that their pain and fear and anxiety that didn't receive attention funnels down through the generations and lands in the heart of the most sensitive child. That child is probably you. You can receive this as a burden, or you can hear it as the gift of being able to bring consciousness to pain and witness the miracles and openings that result from that loving attention. If every dancing particle of pain can be transformed into poetry or art or tears or a growing spot of compassion for others, then every particle is a gift.

How we fear grief. But there is really nothing to fear. When my sons cry so hard they lose their breath, and I can see them trying to get away from their pain, I hold them close and whisper in their ear, "It's okay to feel sad. It's only energy. It will pass through you. I've got you. I'm here." When rewiring the inner pathways from avoiding pain to moving toward it, I often invite my clients to place a hand on their heart and say out loud, "I want to feel my feelings. I'm ready to feel my feelings. It's safe to feel my feelings." This sends the message that you're ready to reverse the lifetime habit of avoiding pain. You can then speak to yourself the way you might speak to a child: "I'm here. I've got you. You're okay."

When you do stop and make time to open to another rhythm, you can enter the grief place. And then particles thaw out and they shimmer with light. And we realize then, when we've cried a small river of wordless tears, when we wake up the next morning and feel a ray of sun in the soul after the storm, when there's a lightness to our step, that the grief place is also the joy place. We know then that grief and joy live in the same chamber of the heart. We know grief is not something to be feared, but that it is the pathway to the peace we all seek.

PRACTICE MEMORIES AND BELIEFS ABOUT PAIN

The first, and most essential, step to feeling the difficult feelings that live in the heart is to make time for them. Grief is like an animal that has been encroached upon by human domination: vulnerable, shy, afraid of the pace and sound of our fast and loud life. In order to make contact, we need to approach slowly and gently with a true desire to listen and learn.

The minute you consider slowing down, a litany of reasons may arise about why that's impossible. This is resistance at work, and it must be named and called to the mat if you're going to move forward with your healing. Notice if any of the following sound familiar.

- I don't have time.

- I should be there for others first.

- Feelings aren't important enough
  (I'm not important enough).

- It's self-centered to take time for
  myself and for inner work.

- I should be able to handle everything; I
  shouldn't need downtime or "being" time.

Remember: if you refuse to make time for your deepest
self to emerge, the self makes itself known in other
ways. This is when you find yourself trapped by intrusive
thoughts, anxiety, or burnout. You go and do and achieve
and burn the candle at both ends, and eventually you
collapse. It's not a sustainable model. And then you're no
good to anyone.

When you're ready to slow down, find a quiet space
when you have a wide swath of time, and reflect on your
first memory of shutting down your pain. This might be
when someone shamed you for crying, with words like,
"Get over it." It might be when you were left alone to
cry. It might be when your parents divorced and nobody
made time for your grief. Allow yourself to time travel
back to that experience with your loving inner parent
traveling with you. Describe the experience in detail in
your journal. Identify the messages that you received
about pain.

Now see your loving inner parent holding that young
you and listen to what she says. What did you want a
grown-up to say or do in that moment of deep pain?
Whatever it is, see your loving inner parent doing and
saying that now. This is how we re-parent our scared, sad
selves. This is how we heal anxiety at the root. ✒

How Unshed Grief Morphs into Anxiety

For years, I dreamed every spring that I was with my grandparents or grieving the loss of them, and I would wake up with the weight of unshed and unarticulated grief sinking my bones. If I didn't have a spacious morning, I couldn't drop into the dream, and would instead jump into the tasks of the day: snuggling my little ones, washing the cat bowl and filling it with fresh food as I noticed the snow or sun on our yard, making breakfast. The sounds and movements of the day began, and the dream was lost in the ether of that other realm.

But the dream wasn't lost at all. It lived beneath the surface, swimming in the current of psyche that had no words, in a slow, quiet world of grief and heartache, loss and longing. But the dream didn't disappear simply because I chose not to carve out time for it. Instead, it created a pane of glass between me and my loved ones. It closed the petals of my heart. It sat, waiting like a child that needed attention. If I failed to notice, it would make itself known in other ways, like morphing into anxiety.

On one of these mornings several years ago, I found myself overfocusing on the fact that Asher, then five, had been tugging on his ear a lot. We knew that he had a buildup of wax, but my grief-laden heart turned anxious mind created a story that morning that he had a swollen lymph node that was the precursor to child leukemia. I had enough presence of mind to resist the dreaded Googling, but I left for my yoga class with the anxious thought that something was terribly wrong. Before I walked out the door, I whispered my worries to my husband, who looked at me like I was crazy. We had just had Asher's well-visit checkup, and we knew everything was fine. But my anxious mind didn't agree.

Once at yoga, I stepped onto my mat and breathed. I scanned my body and became aware of the anxiety, aware of my closed heart, aware of the lack of clarity and joy that normally resided in my soul when the channels were unimpeded by unshed feelings. "Is something awry with work? My marriage? My kids? Am I feeling the challenge of Asher's frequent emotional outbursts? That must be it. No. Doesn't fit; it came from my head." I kept breathing, kept moving, kept sweating.

And then I see her: my grandmother, pruning her prized roses, standing in the dirt on the rise in the backyard of their Santa Monica home, which my grandfather built. The majority of the garden is my grandfather's domain and comes alive with dozens of fruits and vegetables year-round, but the roses are hers. I'm twenty-one. I've just graduated from college. She's teaching me about the roses, showing me where to cut. "Just below the third thorn," she says. She picks a yellow one and two baby pink ones. She gives one to me. We're happy.

Ten years later, I'm standing at those same roses, but she's no longer with me. I'm at her memorial. The backyard is overflowing with their friends and family. I feel like a part of me has been removed, never to return: a petal of my heart that held our love.

The pain lives in my hips, in the spaces between my vertebrae, in my breath. It emerges when I slow down enough to release the memories from my body, where they rise up like apparitions waiting to be seen. She had surgery in March 2003, a procedure that we thought would prolong her life for several more years. My first words to her when she woke up were, "You're going to meet your first great-grandchild!" for nothing would have brought her more joy. She went back into the hospital the night before Passover, and we had the meal without her. It was a quiet meal; my grandfather, normally chatty and jovial at family events, sat slumped in his chair and didn't utter a word. Three weeks later, on April 22, my husband and I were awakened by the phone call that announced her death. I screamed into the pillow and cried from a pain I had never known.

The body remembers, which is why the memories begin in dreams every spring. It always takes me a few days to realize what's happening, and if I don't bring consciousness to the grief and allow myself to cry through another layer of loss, the grief morphs into anxiety or irritation. But as soon as the floodgates open and I allow the tears to wash my soul clean and connect me to the great love I have for my grandmother, the anxiety and irritation dissipate.

I returned home from yoga that day and hugged my kids with an open heart. And, with complete clarity, I knew that Asher was fine.

Turn to Face Your Fear

Grief and sadness aren't the only things we avoid. We run from any uncomfortable feeling, including fear, which can also morph into anxiety. In fact, we can spend our entire lives running from fear. We run from the bear chasing us in the dream. We run from the vague sense of discomfort that seems to follow us on a day spent alone, in silence, away from the distractions of crowds and noise. We run from the things that scare us most, be they flying, public speaking, or intimate relationships.

It's natural to run from fear. It's pure instinct to run from the wild animals and places that lurk in the underbrush of consciousness. We could say it's the most primal instinct of all for species to hide or run in the face of fear. But, interestingly, one of the paths to emotional freedom is facing the inner landscapes that scare us most.

Several years ago, when I attended a dream workshop with dream worker Jeremy Taylor, one of the most fascinating elements discussed was how our unconscious—through the gift of our dream life—invites us to turn and face our fears. One woman shared an archetypal dream about a bear chasing her. The group, most of whom were well-versed in dream work, encouraged her to engage in an active imagination dialogue with the bear and ask it what it wanted. "What is it that you want to share with me?" or "How can I help you?" are important questions to ask the "scary" figures in our dreams. Although paradoxical to the ego, the theory here is that when we stop running from the figures and instead turn to face them, we realize that they are actually here to help us.

Jeremy Taylor shares a fascinating dream in his book *The Wisdom of Your Dreams* that illustrates this point quite poignantly. In a recurring dream, a man is being chased by a fiery dragon, and in a moment of lucidity he turns around and demands to know why the dragon is terrorizing him. The dragon telepathically responds, "I am your smoking addiction!" Taylor shares the dreamer's description:

> In that moment of lucid realization, the dragon
> suddenly seems to change. It doesn't really look any

different, but its "expression" seems to change. It begins to look winsome, almost charming—"Puff, the magic dragon"—more like a big, old familiar, friendly family dog than a menacing, deadly fire-breather.

My lucidity allows me to look even more closely at the "transformed" monster, and I see clearly that there is a nasty, sticky brown slime covering its entire body, and that noxious smoke is oozing and sputtering from every orifice, even from around its eyes, and from under and between its scales. I smell this awful, rancid, repulsive odor coming from it. My revulsion returns, and in the dream, I look at it and say with all my heart, "Get away from me! I no longer want you in my life!"

When he awakened, Alex was amazed to discover that he no longer craved the sensation of smoke in his lungs. Perhaps even more important, the desire for the instant and reliable "companionship" that smoking had always given him was also gone. He has not smoked since the dream.

This story leads us to ask the question: Is our fear, like anxiety, actually a helper in disguise? If you've ever turned to face your fear, you know that it's often by riding directly into the middle of the fear-storm that we grow the most; that, in fact, when we walk through fear, we often have a direct, felt sense of the divine. Since we are no longer sent into the middle of the forest alone for a vision quest, I imagine that fear, and especially panic, are the modern spiritual warrior's training grounds. This means that every moment of fear—especially our greatest fears—provides an opportunity to heighten our capacity to love. This means that every time we can walk through the portal of fear or panic, we discover our true self on the other side.

Fundamental Human Feelings:
Boredom and Loneliness

Boredom

Several times a week my kids will say to me, "I'm bored."

My response is always the same: "Good."

"Why is that good?" they ask.

"Because boredom is a part of life, like loneliness, sadness, happiness, excitement, frustration, and disappointment. And when you let yourself feel bored, something new will arise."

With the proliferation of technology that fills every empty or bored moment with stimulation, our ability to tolerate boredom is a dying skill. Like letter writing and reading actual books (as opposed to digital books), it's a skill that I seek to impart to my kids so that they grow up without needing to fill the boredom with technology (or the variety of stimulants that will be available to them as adults: food, alcohol, drugs, spending money, sex).

Without fail, when I don't rush to cure their boredom and instead let them sit with it for a while, they find something creative to do. I remember one particular time when my younger son was lying on his bed, looking at a fairy house that he had purchased with his birthday money a couple of months before. He said something about how boring it was. It was a lovely, ceramic piece with beautiful colors and interesting designs, but it didn't "do" anything flashy; that wasn't the point. The point was to engage with a piece of art and, perhaps, allow it to lead to imaginary play. I didn't say much in response to his comment. Instead, I quietly engaged in my own activity while peering up occasionally to watch him move from boredom to curiosity about the fairy house. He tapped it and turned it. He held it and touched it. I had no idea what was going through his eight-year-old head; it didn't matter. What mattered was that he was crossing the bridge from boredom to engagement on his own. A piece of learning that he could tolerate boredom was dropping into the puzzle of his psyche. Within twenty minutes his focus had shifted, and he shared what was going through his mind while he was playing with the fairy house: "Mommy, the fairy house is hollow so they could have made the door open.

That would have made it more fun. Why are the windows tinted? I like lying down while I hold it on my chest, because I pretend that I'm tiny and this is my fairy house. Ding-dong. Is anyone home? Hello!"

It was the stream of consciousness of a mind free enough to wander through the fields of an imaginary world. It was a mind unfettered by technology, and a soul with enough empty space to dream. It was a heart that hadn't been hardened over by the onslaught of insults and mean-ness that populate most popular media. His statement showed who we all are underneath the defenses, the intrusive thoughts, the worry, the rumination: our own inner child who is waiting to be set free.

As we talked about in the previous chapter, because we weren't taught how to sit with these uncomfortable states, we learned to travel up to the mind. Here's an example from a client of how the raw feeling of boredom mutates into an intrusive thought: "At least a dozen times a day I have the thought, *I want a different life*. By different I mean not with my husband but with some fantasy guy that will make me feel alive and worthy."

"How do you respond to that thought?"

"I usually try to douse it with some truth-water and say something like, 'Yes, that's your old single self that needs to grieve. And it's okay to feel jealous and want a different life.'"

"How's that response working?"

"It's not."

At this point, I remind my client that she's already grieved the single life plenty of times. If this was the first time I was speaking with her, I would say, "Yes, do your grief work. Write the letters to your single self and ritualize them in some way (burn, rip, dissolve)." But this client has gone down that road a hundred times. Now it's time to go deeper, which means she doesn't need to meet the thought at the level of thoughts. After we splash the thought with cooling cognitive truth, the problems of our thoughts taking over can't be met with more thoughts. We must go deeper.

I guided this client through the steps of breaking free from intru-sive thoughts (see "Practice: Four Steps for Dismantling Intrusive Thoughts" in chapter 9):

"The first step is to name that thought as intrusive. Once you name it, you've created a space between you and the thought. You need to say something like, 'This is my escape-hatch fantasy. It's not my truth even though it feels like my truth in this moment. I am addicted to this escape fantasy because I don't want to feel the messiness of being human.' And remind yourself over and over again that we can't escape the messiness of being human."

"What am I trying to escape?" my client asked.

"Your feelings. Not the feelings that are attached to your intrusive thought and that you project onto your husband, but your core, fundamental feelings of being human: loneliness, boredom, emptiness." (We had discussed earlier in the session how she was feeling bored and empty in her life lately.)

"So all the mental torture is because I don't want to let myself feel that one moment of boredom?" she asked, with more than a little skepticism in her voice.

"Amazingly, yes. It's harder than we think to let ourselves feel that moment of boredom or emptiness without wanting to escape. When we really let ourselves feel it, it's a death moment. It doesn't last, of course, and the more we practice breathing into our painful moments, the easier they become. But we really have to train ourselves to do that, because it's human habit and cultural conditioning to run from those moments. And there are a million ways to run these days. So the question really is: Am I willing to experience the messiness of being human?"

The practice is to name, over and over again, the anxious thoughts, then slow down and rewind until you arrive at the original emotion you were trying to escape from. As my client said, it's hard to believe that a micromoment of boredom could lead to a hamster wheel of intrusive thoughts. But when you remember how deeply conditioned we are to run from emotional pain, it makes sense. The wound of anxiety leads us into the realm of the heart, where we have an opportunity to evolve our emotional consciousness, not only for ourselves but for the culture at large. Every moment you can meet your difficult feelings with kindness is a moment of peace.

Loneliness

Loneliness is another fundamental human emotion that tends to get sidelined by our various addictions (including mental addictions like intrusive thoughts). Because we don't learn that we can tolerate loneliness, we develop a habit in our neural pathway system that hijacks the discomfort the moment it arrives. In fact, we're so averse to loneliness that most people don't even know when they're feeling it or that it's normal to feel it. As a blog reader once commented on one of my posts about loneliness: "This is a bit of an aha post for me. I've always thought of loneliness, boredom, and emptiness as pathologies. Maybe because I have felt them more than most people. My heart always sinks when people say: 'Well, I've not really felt that lonely.' So I think: It *is* only me?"

It's not only you. In fact, it isn't possible to live in this culture without feeling lonely, yet because of our cultural obsession with putting on a happy face, this is yet another taboo topic that nobody discusses. Let's sink into it now.

There's a fundamental loneliness that is part of the fabric of being human. It arrives in the corners of night, when shadows form from curtain folds and the backs of chairs. It seeps in just before twilight, when afternoon exhales its last breath, and evening hasn't yet inhaled. It lives on the edges of exaltation, in the space between the golden hour when the gods breathe their jeweled breath over meadows, and in the splintered crack just before night's multicolored ink begins to sink into dreams.

There are acute times when loneliness appears. Holidays, transitional ebbs in the day or week, birthdays. This is often when the shame stories bleed into loneliness and tell you things like "Everyone else is having fun right now. Everyone else has a family and is off on an adventure, and I'm alone." Or, "I'm not alone—I'm with my family or my partner—and I still feel lonely." Loneliness is the twin sister to grief, and they often arrive at your doorstep, holding hands. When you breathe deeply enough into the loneliness, the dam that has been holding back your grief breaks, and the water comes pouring out on the rivers of memory. First heartbreak. Parents' divorce long ago. A friendship that came to the end of a road.

But loneliness often arrives first, standing with a bouquet of wilted flowers, asking only one thing: to be invited inside. Loneliness arrives like a hollow place in the tree of body, the empty space where diaphragm and stomach meet. Loneliness is the space without breath. Loneliness is the time you cried alone on your bed, and nobody came to comfort you.

There was a time when you were as close to oneness as you could be with another human being, when you grew inside your mother's belly, eating what she ate, smelling what she smelled, moving as she moved. But even then, there was an amniotic sac that surrounded you and created a definable boundary between baby and mother. There is still a sac. We can no longer see it, but this white slippery sac of separateness surrounds us still. We are meant to feel lonely. It's part of the definition of being human.

It's important to know this so that we don't fall into traps of thinking it should be otherwise. The culture sends us both overt and covert messages that it should be otherwise; that if you lose weight or live in this house or have this baby with this partner, you will be immunized against loneliness. It isn't so.

There isn't a partner in the world that can protect you against loneliness. That's not the function of love.

There isn't a friend in the world that can protect you against loneliness. That's not the reason for friendship.

There isn't a child in the world that can protect you from loneliness. That's not the purpose of being a parent.

There is only one antidote to loneliness: to befriend it. When we make friends with loneliness—shedding the belief that we're not supposed to feel it and shattering the fantasy that other people with their families and friends are immune to it—we welcome it in through the front door. We greet loneliness as we would any other feeling state and become curious about its stories. "Loneliness," we might say, "tell me about yourself. What color are you? What shape are you? What stories from my past live in the strands of yarn that compose your tattered blankets?"

Once you invite loneliness inside, it changes tenor. This is the paradox of loneliness: when we befriend it, it shape-shifts. It's still there, in the pocket of your body, but it loses its spike. Once you invite loneliness over the threshold, it softens, like an angry child taken into a mother's warm arms. Curiosity is the potion that shifts it, and creativity is the medicine that sends it into channels of light.

On the other side of loneliness is solitude. When you sink into loneliness without fighting it, solitude will reach for your hand and invite you into endless conversation, leading you down the grassy pathways and dimly lit cobblestone streets that make up the labyrinth of your soul. In this place, there is no more loneliness. You no longer long for someone to sit beside you on the bench, because you are in the timeless place where creativity and imagination enrapture you in their ways. Once you have surrendered, you find that you could stay there for a very long time. And you discover that with a full cup, you see your life and your partner and your child and your friends through a very different lens. They are no longer here to fill you up but are vessels into which you can pour your light. The fullness of self leads to the fullness of love. We walk through the doorways that scare us, and we find ourselves waiting with a bouquet of brilliant flowers on the other side.

11

LONGING

Where the lips are silent the heart has a thousand tongues.

RUMI
The Book of Love: Poems of Ecstasy and Longing

Longing, like anxiety, is a messenger, and because it's so often misunderstood and taken at face value, it deserves its own chapter. We typically feel longing like an ache for more—more money, more children, more excitement, more connection—and if we read the "more" at the surface level, we miss the wisdom of the longing. Longing is a signal pointing to unmet needs, unshed grief, and unlived dreams and, as such, is an invitation to deepen our relationship to each of the four realms of self. Longing, like anxiety, pulls us toward wholeness. When we place longing on our radar and stop taking it at face value, we can begin to decipher its messages. In order to do this, we must learn to discern between root longing and secondary longing.

Root Versus Secondary Longing

Longing, like anxiety, is rarely talked about and profoundly misunderstood, and when it is discussed it is almost exclusively in the context of sex and unrequited love. Because of our cultural obsession with romantic love (see chapter 15), the moment longing tinges the heart, we assume it has to do with love. Yet the longings that clients bring to sessions tell a very different, and much more interesting, story. They share:

- I long for a baby.
- I long for a partner.
- I long for my mother.
- I long for my father.
- I long for the parents I never had.
- I long for my childhood.
- I long for a house.
- I long for community.
- I long for a best friend.
- I long for God (or spirit, connection to something higher, whatever term works for you).
- I long for a different climate.
- I long for a different city.
- I long to be single.
- I long to feel alive.
- I long to feel in love.
- I long to feel desire.

What composes the hymn of longing? What notes make up the sonata that stirs the soul like a great piece of music, rising up from the depths of self, commanding our attention until we listen intently?

Until we decipher its code and learn its language, how to meet the longing remains a mystery, and we often confuse root longing with secondary longing. Root longing calls our attention to a whole and real need inside that, when met, can point us toward a new direction or experience in life. Secondary longing contains whispers of a root longing that must be deciphered so that we don't follow signs that point us in a misguided direction.

For example, the longing for spirit is a root longing. When we feel that longing, there's nothing to decipher or decode; we must simply listen and learn how to bring more of a connection to spirit into our lives. When my clients sit in church and describe the longing that arises as they listen to the music and gather in community, that's a healthy, root longing that says, "This feeds my soul. I need more of this. Listen."

The longing for father, on the other hand, is primarily a second-ary longing. If you didn't grow up with a healthy, loving father figure, the longing for one often arises during adulthood. This longing, when unexamined, can then lead a woman to seek relationships with older men as a way to try to fulfill the absence. This never works and only leads to more longing. To break apart this secondary longing is to arrive at the core longing, which can contain a longing for spirit, and also a longing for one's own clear, masculine, inner father—the part of you that can make decisions, set boundaries, and execute plans in the world.

The same is true with the longing for mother. Many people who were raised by a narcissistic mother suffer from a mother wound, which leads them to seek false mother figures or project their unworked feel-ings about this primal relationship onto their partner. When we break apart the longing and examine the wound at its core, we find grief at the center: the grief of not having had a mother who knew how to put your needs first. This needs attention. Then there is the invi-tation to create a sustaining, daily relationship with both the Great Mother, through nature and active imagination, and with one's own inner mother: the part of you that tends to yourself with compassion and gentleness. If you only follow the original longing, you miss the deeper underpinnings that can guide you toward healing and growth.

We can deconstruct the list of longings at the beginning of this chapter in the same manner. Some of the longings—like the longing for a baby—contain both a root longing and a secondary long-ing. When a woman longs for a baby, we must take it at face value, because becoming a mother is one of the most primal needs for many women. But when conception doesn't occur quickly, she's then asked to deconstruct this immense longing into its disparate elements. There, she often finds a longing for her own wholeness and a need to connect to the fertility of being a fully creative woman that extends beyond conception.

If we are to be love-warriors, we must find the courage to meet all our emotions with tenderness and curiosity, understanding that they originate inside us and, thus, can be resolved inside of us. The culturally conditioned habit is to jump ship when longing arises and fall prey to the belief that the answers lie "out there." The love-warrior stays the course and turns inward to discover the true source of longing.

There is wisdom in longing, a message from the underworld of psyche that longs to be known. If we take longing at face value, we often find ourselves on a wild goose chase punctuated by increasing anxiety that culminates in despair. But when we learn to read the impulses from psyche as messages from the underworld and avail ourselves of the archetype of Persephone, the goddess who goes between the worlds of seen and unseen, we become our own wise woman or wise man, our own oracle that can divine our paths without needing to seek answers from other so-called experts. For contained in the messages of longing, like anxiety and intrusive thoughts, are pearls of wisdom that, when deciphered, can lead us onto our own empowered path, where we deeply know what we need to know, and where we uncover the ungrieved loss and unlived lives that need our attention.

The Lives We Will Never Live

We only live one life, and we make choices along the way that, by the very definition of making one choice, exclude and shut the door to other choices. The roads not taken and the lives not lived need attention, otherwise they collect layers of dust in the warehouse of psyche and make themselves known through the great sneeze of anxiety and its symptoms.

This truth was punctuated for me one day, many years ago, when I was leaving my son's wheel-throwing class and I struck up a conversation with one of the other moms. She had two daughters who attended the class, and I asked the basic questions such as, "How old are they? Where do you live?" The girls went to retrieve their coats from the cubbyholes, and there was something about the way they joked with each other that sent a small, almost imperceptible pang of longing through me. I could have easily brushed it aside. But I didn't. As soon as we walked into the icy air and crunched our boots into the snow, the thought appeared in my mind, "I'll never raise sisters."

It wasn't the first time this longing had appeared. When we learned that our second baby was a boy, I celebrated and grieved. I had always imagined that I would have a daughter, so after our first son was born, I still held out hope that our second would be a girl. But he wasn't, and as I lay in bed that day after receiving the test results that revealed the sex of our unborn baby, I lay also with the awareness that I would never raise a daughter. I don't remember crying. I do remember rolling around the phrase, "I'm the mother of sons" in my mind and trying to adjust. But I have cried since then, knowing that it's through the grieving that acceptance arrives.

Needing to attend to my kids after the pottery class, I filed the longing away under *L* in the Rolodex of my soul and trusted that, in a slowed-down moment, it would resurface to receive the attention it needed.

Later that evening, I felt it bubble back up, and my ego-mind stumbled for a moment on a quick and fruitless litany of what-ifs—"What if I had made a different choice here or there?"—as a way to avoid the rawness of the longing. This was my small mind's obviously futile attempt to control the past and avoid the vulnerable and unpredictable realm of feeling by keeping me trapped in the thatched pattern of thoughts that dead-ends in a chain-link fence. I stayed there for less than a second before I opened the fence and walked into the field of feelings, letting myself sink down, go in, shift out of my head, and breathe into my heart.

Then the grief flowed through. In an instant, I knew it wasn't only the grief of not being able to experience what it's like to raise a girl or sisters but also the grief about not having a third child. We had decided to close the door at two, and while the choice was loving for our family, there was still a pain that pricked my heart every so often. And there it was, making its way up the riverways of sweet grief that bent and curved from heart to soul to eyes. The surrender to pure pain is always sweet. We fight it, the engrained habits of another era or another stage creating resistance to the pain, but once the fortress falls away, there's a smile attached to the tears. Sweet release, sweet opening inside, sweet tears clearing out the pain and transforming the longing into gratitude.

It's easy to fall prey to the belief that longing necessitates action: If I occasionally long for a third child, it means I have to *have* a third child. Or if I long for a daughter, it means I have to have a daughter. Part of the growth process involves being able to hold a feeling without immediately resolving it, trusting that resolution occurs with no action other than conscious holding and tending to the feelings. We also mistakenly conclude that every feeling that passes through our field of consciousness is an unarguable and blanket truth. We don't understand that we can feel longing without it being the final truth. In other words, I can sporadically long for a daughter, but my deeper truth is that two children—*these* two boys—complete our family.

The work, thus, is always the same: make room for the pain, move toward it, welcome it, love it, *and* orient toward the beauty and gratitude. I wrote that story in my head years ago while lying next to my unbelievably precious boy (almost five years old at the time): the one who makes my heart feel like it's going to explode from love every day, the one who makes my soul sing, the one who fills me with unimaginable joy. I often hear my clients say things like, "But if I allow myself to long for [something else], doesn't that mean I don't love or appreciate my current [partner, child, parent]?" No, it doesn't mean that at all. The seasoned mind can hold the polarities.

In fact, being able to adopt a both/and approach is one of the hallmarks of maturity and an antidote to anxiety. The world isn't a black-and-white place. The ego-mind believes that if we categorize every experience, we will feel more in control. We can categorize our spices and organize our clothes, but the realm of the heart-mind is often a messy place that defies categorization. The best we can do is make room for the apparent opposites, to hold them both as true while knowing that one doesn't invalidate the other. I can experience a moment of longing for a daughter while celebrating with immense gratitude my two sons. I can allow myself to long for the experience of raising sisters while relishing the adventure of witnessing the complex layers of my boys' relationship to each other (and you better believe I'm banking on granddaughters). I can grieve and celebrate, lose and love, long and feel grateful. There's room for it all.

The Wisdom of Longing

I'll share another story of what it looks like to breathe into the present-ing pang of longing and spiral into its wisdom.

Several years ago, over the span of several weeks, I felt a subtle pang of longing every time a luxury, high-end car passed me. The obvious, first-layer interpretation was that I was longing for a nicer car, but I knew immediately that that wasn't it. I'm not a car person, and I'm perfectly content with the functional, safe car that I drive.

Breathe. Go deeper.

The second-layer interpretation was that I was longing for more money, as represented by the luxury sedan.

Not it. Money is fine. Go deeper.

The third-layer interpretation was that I was longing for more stability. Often the fancy car would be driven by a distinguished gen-tleman in his seventies, and I could feel the quivery ache of longing for the patriarch of our family who would handle things, someone who would provide the pillar of protection and wisdom as the stable trunk of our family tree.

Close. Getting deeper. Shine the light of consciousness directly on the pain.

And then I knew. It emerged from the core of my soul, the heart of my heart. It was the longing for a family home, the grief from the loss of my childhood house after my parents' divorce. It was longing for the older generation to wrap me in its embrace and feed me at its table, the longing to feel taken care of by elders, held in the greater web of an intergenerational community.

My eyes welled up with tears. I breathed into the grief brought forth by my longing. There was nothing to do with it, nothing to fix. Further wisdom arrived a few days later, a life-changing insight that we, my husband and I, and our home were the family hub now. We could offer this, and in the offering, the ache of the longing was diminished. But at the moment when the wisdom of the long-ing pierced consciousness, I simply stayed with the opening of pain, purified by the light of awareness instead of encased inside the long-ing. And once I broke open to the root pain, the superficial longing disappeared completely.

I don't know why psyche communicates in symbol and code. Wouldn't it be easier if we could understand ourselves without having to do the detective work of deciphering the messages? Yes, it would, but arguing with the way psyche communicates is as futile as arguing against reality. For some reason, we're not meant to land on the big answers directly. We are invited, instead, to spiral into wisdom, to learn our secret codes only by spending slow time with ourselves. We learn to love our hidden communications. As Pablo Neruda writes, "as certain dark things are to be loved, in secret, between the shadow and the soul."

PRACTICE BECOMING CURIOUS ABOUT LONGING

Next time you notice the pang of longing, become curious about its embedded messages. Ask yourself if it's root longing or secondary longing, while remembering that the anxious mind can easily attach to the first-layer interpretation and run with it, which will almost invariably exacerbate your anxiety. Instead, imagine that your longing is a hand, and when you take it, you're led into the underlayers of self. Allow curiosity to be your guide and patience to be your friend. You're not looking for answers so much as signposts, and when you follow these signposts, you'll be led to your wisdom. To follow these signposts, loosely follow these suggestions:

1. When you notice the feeling of longing, name it as longing. Notice what it feels like in your body. Where do you feel longing? If you could describe it as a metaphor or image, what would that be?

2. Send your breath directly into the longing. Imagine that your breath is visible and you can see it wrap itself around the longing.

3. As you continue to breathe deeply and consciously, ask yourself: What is the core longing beneath this top-layer longing? It might take time to arrive at the core longing, but you'll know when you land on it from the aha feeling in your body and the feeling of grief that arises.

4. Allow the feelings to move through you and give them creative expression if you feel inspired: draw, paint, dance, write a poem.

12

THE REALM OF SOUL

> Everything has become speeded up and
> overcrowded. So everything that slows us down
> and forces patience, everything that sets us back
> into the slow cycles of nature, is a help.
>
> **MAY SARTON**
> *Journal of a Solitude*

May Sarton wrote the above quote in 1973. How much faster and more crowded our world has become since then! One of the key messages embedded in anxiety is a call from soul to slow down, to clear out, to come home. Soul does not move at technological time; it moves at the rhythm of nature, whose pace has remained constant since the beginning of time. Both the presence of anxiety and a sense of numbness are strong indicators of a parched soul. It's as if the soul is saying, "I can't hear myself think. I can't connect. I can't breathe. Please stop *doing* and step into *being*."

The Well of Being

One morning, when I was getting ready to leave for a family gathering, the term "well-being" popped into my head. It's a term we hear a lot these days, especially if we frequently use resources that promote a healthy lifestyle. And I thought, "Well-being. A well of being. Well-being means that you're able to access a *well of being* inside of you."

There may be no medicine more effective to neutralize anxiety than accessing your own well of being, the quiet resting place inside where you can hear the noise of your mind settle down and physically feel your soul relax. It's your own private retreat that's accessible and free. It's what the Buddhists call refuge, often in reference to our tendency to seek comfort in fleeting external objects and conditions instead of the sustainable inner realm. It's a well whose waters are filled by nourishing acts of non-doing, also known as *being*.

There are so many ways to fill the time and space these days, endless distractions that draw us away with magnetic pull from the inner world. Anything you do that externalizes your sense of self depletes the waters of your well of being. This includes spending time on social media with the intention of avoiding yourself and real connection with live people; watching too many mindless movies; staying busy by completing tasks on your endless to-do lists; giving in to the cravings of addictions (including the mental addictions of ruminating, obsessing, and worrying); scrolling, clicking, texting, staring, binging, gaming, posting.

We all spend time engaging in acts that externalize self, and, in balance, some of these actions are essential to a different kind of well-being. But when the external far outweighs the internal, or the external isn't balanced on a daily basis with real time spent inward in nourishing ways, it begins to take a toll and anxiety ramps up. Thus, it requires a strong commitment, an ironclad decision to learn how to turn off screens and other forms of externalization and turn toward the quieter, slower ways.

The way to grow your well of being is exactly as the term suggests: you learn to cultivate a relationship to *being*. Being is non-doing, and it's beyond non-doing. You could say that you're "doing nothing" when you're stretched out on the couch watching television. And while this may help you unwind after a long day, it doesn't fill the well with nourishing waters. For most people, watching TV or surfing the internet are not simply acts of unwinding but ways to check out by avoiding the inner world.

True *being* is a quiet, still, often solitary place without distractions. It's a feminine energy. It's reflective and inward, qualities inhabited by the night, the moon, water, darkness. It's slow, compassionate, soft, curious, and without agenda. It's slower than slow, in fact; it's timeless. It's everything our modern world and our modern self are lacking.

In order to create a well of being, we need daily, weekly, monthly, and yearly retreats. Some people call these windows of inwardness a Sabbath or a day of rest, which is the original intention of a weekend. As Rabbi David Cooper writes in *Renewing Your Soul*:

> Modern civilization suffers from a chronic condition of anemic, starving souls. The sages teach us that if we feed our souls, we will experience a new kind of happiness and more meaning in life. They say we will see nature more clearly and a new world of inner peace will open. Renew the soul and one's perspective of daily life will completely change. It is simply a matter of taking time, slowing down, shifting mundane consciousness into realms of higher insight, giving oneself the gift of reflection and contemplation.

How do you fill the inner well? There are many paths, and what works for someone else may not work for you. But deep inside, you have a sense of what opens your heart, what connects you to the deeper flow of life force or vitality, places and actions that help you turn inward and fill you with a sense of calm and connection to the realm of soul. As you read through the following words, notice that sense of yes, then take the actions each day that nourish your soul.

- Offering gratitude
- Recording and tending to dreams
- Fresh air and sunshine
- Smiling at a stranger
- Gardening
- Beauty, flowers, color, trees
- Sitting near a body of water, or immersing yourself in one

- Walking and talking with a close friend
- Taking the long way home
- Meandering
- Encountering a wild animal
- Pets
- Reading a poem, and writing one
- Drawing, painting, writing, dancing, singing, chanting
- Being in nature
- Autumn colors, snowfall, spring buds
- Walking in the rain
- Talking to the moon
- Looking at the stars
- Listening to crickets
- Candlelight
- Baths
- Stillness, silence, and solitude
- Doing less and being more
- Being in silence
- Meaningful rituals

As you can see, none of these actions or experiences require spending money, getting in your car, or even much time. The paths to your soul are free and always accessible to you, and your anxiety is pointing the way.

The Essential Function of Healthy Rituals

The soul needs healthy rituals in order to stay well nourished. For most of human history, people have engaged in time-honored rituals to walk them through the tenuous thresholds of milestones and transitions when the veil between the worlds is thinner and we're more aware of the passage of time, change, loss, and death. Sensitive children and then adults are aware of how vulnerable we are at these thresholds—and in the entire threshold of life. Without a healthy tether to ground and anchor, the soul feels adrift, and we turn to obsessions and compulsions as a way to hold on to and create an illusion of control. These obsessions and compulsions may manifest outwardly in the form of checking that doors are locked and stoves are off, or inwardly in the form of mental obsessions like seeking endless reassurance on the internet for the current hook that your anxiety is hanging its hat on.

While the culture likes to diagnose these obsessions and compulsions as indicators of a disorder, I see these symptoms as indicators that there's something unspeakably beautiful inside: a soul of such exquisite sensitivity lost in a world that doesn't value its beauty, so it is left to find anchors in the only ways it knows how. What we call compulsive rituals are spiritual sensitivity gone awry: the ego's attempt to control something bad from happening and define an uncertain future.

What we should have been taught as children, and need to teach our "outer" and inner kids today, is how to find healthy anchors so that we can safely dive into the deep and rich waters of life. The healthy anchors are meaningful rituals, prayers, and poetry that can help you connect to your inner resources of safety, connectedness, and comfort. If you woke up and went to sleep each morning with these elements, your sense of safety and protection would increase, and your anxiety would diminish.

When you connect to meaningful rituals, you connect to something bigger than yourself. Simply slowing down for a few minutes with the intention to turn inward helps you connect to the hum that connects all living beings. This hum is always there. All you need to do is drop underneath the surface of things, risk letting go of the compelling and addictive vine of control and mind-chatter, and you'll find that you can tap into this hum. Ancient peoples have known for thousands of years that rituals connect us to the healthy web and remind us of our place in the world. It's time we excavate that wisdom and meet the root need that's manifesting itself as mental addictions, and thereby honor ourselves at the deepest level possible: the level of soul.

PRACTICE DEVELOPING
HEALTHY RITUALS

Consider what your morning and evening rituals will be, and commit to doing them every day. I suggest creating a simple ritual altar with a candle, a bell or gong, a meaningful photo that inspires you to connect to self, and a couple of sacred objects (shells, rocks, spiritual symbols).

Keep in mind that you can and must create rituals that are aligned with your values and belief system. If you are already grounded in a religious tradition, you have an abundance of rituals from which to choose: you can read spiritual texts, recite prayers, light candles. If you're not religious, don't let the word *ritual* scare you. It simply means a meaningful act that you engage in on a regular basis. We all have rituals that inform our lives, but most of them lack meaning, so they don't serve the function of creating an inner anchor and protection system. We have bedtime rituals, like washing our face, brushing our teeth, putting on our pajamas, but they're more rote routines than actual rituals. Now is the time to create rituals that are aligned with your values.

As you sit before your altar, light a candle, take one or more of the following actions, and watch as your soul receives the nourishment it so desperately needs.

- Read a meaningful quote or spiritual text
  (leaving a book by your altar is helpful).

- Say prayers.

- Breathe.

- Practice mindfulness.

- Say a mantra to help connect you to self-love.

- Listen to an audio track that helps you feel connected (anything from soundstrue.com).

- Memorize a poem.

- Practice yoga.

- Write a gratitude list.

- Write down your dreams.

- Set your intention for the day.

- Open your senses to receive and notice the world around you: listen to the birds singing in the morning or the wind rustling in the trees at night. If you live in a city, see if you can open your heart to the hum of compassion that connects every living being like an invisible web.

The more you begin to implement and incorporate the mindsets and practices I teach throughout this book, the more adept you'll become at tuning into the first niggling of anxiety that taps at your soul, and instead of responding by tightening around it you, you'll be able to turn inward and ask, "What is needed?" Sometimes what's needed is simply to get up, walk outside, and breathe in fresh air. This is the soul saying, "Enough sitting. Enough working. Enough zoning out. I'm starving and I need attention. Let's go sit on the earth, or let's go read a poem." Walking barefoot on the grass or sitting next to flowers can restore the soul in seconds.

Remember: anxiety is your friend, not your enemy. It's a messenger pointing to a need or wound that needs attention inside. The more you respond with curiosity, the more you will heal. And the more you heal, the more you'll be able to bring the gifts of who you really are into the world around you.

13

WHEN ANXIETY HEALS

The final stage of healing is using what happens to
you to help other people. That is healing in itself.

GLORIA STEINEM

W hen you attend to the four realms, you will notice something fascinating: the more you release and refill in
healthy ways, the more a space opens up inside. If you
don't understand the process of healing, you can easily become alarmed
by this space, which can then activate a new round of anxiety. On the
other hand, when you understand that healing, like nature, follows a
cycle, you can make room for the rebirth that invariably arises on the
other side of loss. But first you have to walk through the empty space,
the liminal zone that occupies the second stage of all transitions.

Anxiety and Emptiness

There's a natural and predictable pattern that people experience when
healing from anxiety. The following comment on one of my blog posts
is a sentiment I often hear:

> Sheryl, could you please blog about the "space" that anxiety
> occupies? This is exactly what I'm feeling right now. There's
> nothing wrong; I have nothing to be anxious about. Yet
> there's this sadness and empty feeling. I know it needs my
> attention, but I can't figure out where it's coming from.

Anxiety, like all emotions, is energy. Energy takes up space in your mind and body. When you attend to the anxiety, and it begins to fall away, the space that anxiety previously occupied opens up. What's often left is emptiness, and if you don't fill the emptiness with the next obsessive thought or action, you will notice one or both of the following.

- You'll open a space for clarity and spiritual direction to enter, and/or

- the underlying feelings that you've been covering up your entire life will emerge.

Guided by a culture that encourages them to stay busy and fill up empty time and space, when most people encounter emptiness, they rush to try to figure out what's wrong, and then they usually fill it back up again with the endless chatter of thoughts. Instead of pouring thought into the empty space, I encourage you to simply sit with it, to make a place for the emptiness; instead of resisting the quiet space, resist the cultural belief that says that there's something wrong with emptiness.

Remember that in the three-stage process of transitions—letting go, liminal, rebirth—emptiness is the defining quality of the liminal zone. So it often happens for people who find my work that after they've worked through the initial layers of anxiety and learn that they're not alone, the space opens up for wisdom and pain to enter. And, yes, those two experiences—wisdom and pain—are cousins in the inner world of psyche.

The truth is that it's *only* when we work through the static creating layers of anxiety and arrive at emptiness that we can begin to find our clarity. The emptiness is an essential stage. As Rabbi Tirzah Firestone writes in *With Roots in Heaven*:

> Sometimes the more powerful response is disengagement,
> to simply stop trying to appease this dark angel, to stop
> wrestling—reacting, proving, defending our worth—and
> sit still. By not reacting to our inner beasts, neither fighting

nor trying to disprove them, we create an empty space in ourselves. This empty space of nonaction is critical on the spiritual path. Just as water requires an empty container in which to be collected, so the Self requires an empty space in us in to which to pour its guidance.

When you find yourself on this threshold where the anxiety has quieted and you're left with the emptiness, allow it to be there. If you stop moving and stop searching and find stillness, you'll touch into what wants to be known. You'll grieve, yes. You'll cry out in old pain. You'll find yourself raw and vulnerable. You'll open to wisdom. You'll find clarity. You'll feel joy. It begins with the willingness to keep your heart open and experience whatever has been living beneath the anxiety.

Real life isn't a Hollywood movie; it isn't a two-hour, Technicolor, larger-than-life adventure where every edited moment is alive and exciting. Real life isn't *People* magazine; it isn't a glossy paper anthology with airbrushed photographs adorning the pages. Real life isn't Facebook, a newsreel of snapshots like a window into the highlights of someone else's life. There are moments—seasons even—of emptiness. We don't capture those on film, because they're not very interesting to look at from the outside. But from the inside, if you stop and stay still, you'll find your own inner world, which has been waiting to be known and which is more exciting, real, and interesting than any Hollywood adventure. And if you stay still long enough and continue with your inner work, you'll discover the fruits of your labor.

The Fruits of the Labor

From the emptiness we move toward the next stage of growth, which is the new birth that arises from mining the gems of healing and bringing them into the world in some way. By "into the world" I don't mean in a grand way. I mean in any way that calls you: bringing more compassion to your children (because you've learned to be compassionate with yourself first), bringing more kindness to the earth (because you've learned that you deserve kindness), or following a lifelong dream.

We heal not only for ourselves. It's a starting point, yes, and a very important one, but ultimately, this inner healing naturally ripples outward. The world needs you to do this work. Sometimes when resistance is high and the ego insists on not budging (for example, when a client is having trouble committing to the daily tools required to lead to change), I'll say, "If you can't do it for you, can you do it for your children or your future children?" Extending ourselves for the benefit of another and to stop intergenerational patterns can often inspire people to find the courage to commit to their inner work.

Healing is not navel-gazing. It's not selfish, luxurious, or something "extra" that we do. It's central and essential. It's what our world needs, and it needs it now. It needs each and every one of you to reach into the depths of your soul and find the strength, courage, and commitment to take full responsibility for your pain, learn to work with your thoughts and tend to your feelings, stop waiting for someone else to do it for you or rescue you, and instead step into the power of your path. It's not your mother's job or your father's job to fix your pain. It's not your partner's job to fan the fire of your soul and make you feel alive. It's not your friend's job to hold your pain for you. It's your job and yours alone. And the time is now.

PART THREE

RELATIONSHIPS

When you love someone, you do not love them all the
time, in exactly the same way, from moment to moment.
It is an impossibility. It is even a lie to pretend to. And
yet this is exactly what most of us demand. We have
so little faith in the ebb and flow of life, of love, of
relationships. We leap at the flow of the tide and resist
in terror its ebb. We are afraid it will never return.
We insist on permanency, on duration, on continuity;
when the only continuity possible, in life as in love,
is in growth, in fluidity—in freedom, in the sense
that the dancers are free, barely touching as
they pass, but partners in the same pattern.

ANNE MORROW LINDBERGH
Gift from the Sea

14

THE VULNERABILITY
OF CONNECTION

> We pretend we aren't vulnerable, but this is an illusion.
> We are incarnated in a delicate body, intertwined
> in the community of life. Our senses have evolved
> to be exquisitely tuned to the ever-changing world
> of pleasure and pain, sweet and sour, gain and loss.
> Love and freedom invite us to turn toward the world.
> They offer the gifts of a flexible heart, wide enough
> to embrace experience, vulnerable yet centered.
>
> JACK KORNFIELD

Nowhere does anxiety show up with more intensity and confusion than in our intimate relationships: with friends, colleagues, relatives, and most prominently with partners and children. For if anxiety is often a protector against vulnerable feelings—and nowhere are we more vulnerable than in our relationships—it makes sense that anxiety would have a field day where the heart is most at risk for loss. This is when it's essential to understand the workings of anxiety and decode its message so that we don't become lost in its top-layer manifestations, closing ourselves off from the one thing we crave, need, and long for more than anything else in this world: love.

The vulnerability of loving becomes illuminated in those moments when fear falls away and we gain a clear glimpse into the center of our heart. One of these poignant moments occurred one night many years ago when, through a rare turn of events as a mother of two young children, I was able to attend an evening yoga class with my favorite teacher. The class started at 5:30 p.m., so at 5:00 p.m. I gathered my things, kissed everyone good-bye, and drove into the darkening evening. As I parked, then walked to class, I marveled at the novelty of being out at night: the bare-leaved trees on the Twenty Ninth Street mall adorned with winter lights; couples on first dates strolling on the idyllic promenade; the Rocky Mountains jutting up in the dark blue light behind them; young parents toting their baby from a restaurant to the car, beaming at their little treasure. It had been a long time since I was out at night on my own, and I felt like an alien visiting from another planet, thoroughly enjoying earthly sights.

The class was beautiful. My teacher channeled wisdom, and my body half heard him as I breathed into the poses and allowed his words to trickle in and reverberate on a nonverbal level. Sometimes a phrase would catch my breath like, "We must meet our egos with kindness, as it's not something we can get rid of. The ego is the part of us that must travel on this earth, and because it knows that it cannot accompany us beyond the line of mortality, it holds a sadness. We must meet this sadness with compassion." His words traveled directly to my heart, where I thought first about my then eight-year-old older son and his unfiltered awareness of death, which brought with it a necessary sadness. I thought about how my husband and I continuously met his sadness and helped him find ways of defining it in his body so that it could move through him without causing stagnation. I then thought about my clients who also struggled with an awareness of death as children, and how alone they felt as they tried to process the existential questions without a guide. I opened my heart to the pain, the tenderness, the rawness of being human.

As the class progressed, and the blue evening darkened into black night, I thought about the walk from the studio to my car, which was parked at the far end of the parking lot, and I noticed a jolt of fear flash through me. In my twenties, I used to go out all the time at night and would park in all kinds of strange places. I had certainly felt fear in the past, but I had never had as much to lose as I did that night: a husband whom I adore beyond words and two magical sons who would be crushed if something happened to me. I had more to lose than that, of course, including a tight-knit circle of friends who are like family, but it was the intimate loved ones, the children of my womb, that flashed into my fear-mind as the class came to a close.

I lay down in *Savasana* and breathed into the fear. Within moments, I could feel underneath the fear into the vulnerability of loving my husband and two boys more than I ever knew possible. And with the awareness of the vulnerability, came the tears. They weren't tears of grief; they were tears of rawness, tears that arose from knowing that loving that deeply meant taking an immense risk, and that should anything happen to any one of us, our hearts would be torn apart. Beyond that I could not go, except to hold out a thin strand of faith that should anything occur, somehow, some way, we would mend.

The risk of loving. Oh, it brings me to tears even now as I write these words. The risk of spinning this web of love around the four of us more deeply every day, of opening our hearts wider and wider and wider, until we feel they will break from the loving. But they don't break; they only expand. The love reaches out into worlds beyond our world and asks us to grow beyond ourselves.

Anyone who commits to this path of healing must unravel into the heart of the fear and, at the very center, touch down into the risk of loving. The fears keep us separate from the raw and vulnerable places in our hearts. There are moments when I see with crystalline clarity that the endless questions that show up in romantic love ("Do I love him/her enough?" "What if I'm settling?") and the ways the mind ruminates about other meaningful relationships (with friends and family) are all elaborate defense mechanisms. They are designed to avoid the vulnerability of loving, the exquisitely painful knowledge that when we commit our hearts, we take the risk of enduring the most painful of human experiences: loss and heartbreak.

Sitting at the center of worry and intrusive thoughts is, quite simply, the fear of loss, and if you could peel those thoughts away, you would cry, as I did that night. And through the strength of the tears, you would find the courage to go on, to expose your heart, and take the only risk worth taking: to love and be loved as fully and completely as if it were your last day on earth. To love without restraint. To love with joyous abandon. To set the fear-voices on a fence at the edge of the meadow of your mind and witness them while knowing that they are no longer running the show, allowing them to watch you as you run or dance or stumble into the arms of love.

15

THE ROMANTIC CONNECTION

What my marriage taught me is that real love is only what you give. That's all. Love is not "out there," waiting for you. It is in you. In your own heart: in what you are willing to give of it. We are all capable of love, but few of us have the courage to do it properly. . . . You can take a person's love and waste it. But you are the fool. When you give love, it grows and flowers inside you like a carefully pruned rose. Love is joy. Those who love, no matter what indignities, what burdens they carry, are always full of joy.

KATE KERRIGAN
Recipes for a Perfect Marriage

Not everyone struggles with anxiety in relationships, but for the sensitive, analytical, conscientious people in the world, to experience anxiety and doubt in a committed, loving relationship where there are no red flags (see appendix A) is not only commonplace but predictable. If one of the root causes of anxiety is the need to find certainty and ground in a fundamentally groundless world, and if romantic relationships are the place where we are rendered most vulnerable and, thus, groundless, why would we be surprised when anxiety shows up there? Yet in the absence of accurate information and because of the widespread cultural assumption that doubt means don't, what begins as normal questioning or healthy fear quickly morphs and balloons into full-blown anxiety and panic. We all lack the basic roadmap that can lead to relationship satisfaction and success.

What you're about to receive is the roadmap to healthy love that you never received. We'll extrapolate on one of the basic premises of my work: the often overlooked and misunderstood link between relationships and anxiety. And we will expound upon the following truths: love is not the absence of fear, and it's not a feeling; it's an action and a willingness to wrestle with the fear that arises every time we move toward increased intimacy and commitment with a safe and available partner. Because love and fear are wrestling on the mat of the heart, relationships require us to become nothing short of love-warriors.

What Is Relationship Anxiety?

I define "relationship anxiety" as pervasive doubts about a healthy, loving relationship. It usually begins with a thought like, "Do I love my partner enough?" or "What if I'm not in love or attracted enough?" and spirals from there into a level of anxiety that interferes with your ability to be present in your relationship, and often in your life. Even for those who don't suffer from relationship anxiety, it's a sad reality that our divorce rates have skyrocketed in recent years and that very few couples experience long-term real love and passion. This is often because most of what we learn about relationships from the mainstream culture is false, which means that many people run at the first sign of "falling out of love." In fact, one of the most common reasons that people walk away from loving, solid, healthy relationships is because they say they're not in love anymore: "I love her, but I'm not *in love* with her," is considered a valid reason to leave.

Relationship anxiety generally manifests in two ways, either of which can occur at any point in the relationship, from early on or years into marriage. The first type of relationship anxiety occurs in a defining moment when the thought, "Do I love my partner enough or at all" enters the mind. Prior to this thought, the person describes their relationship as: "Wonderful, loving. Everything I've ever wanted. We have an amazing love between us, and it's pretty much perfect." The couple often had a long honeymoon period and a very healthy relationship. The early stages of this type of relationship anxiety are characterized by the desperate need to "get back the feelings," as the loss of in-loveness feels like their hearts have been cut out of their chests.

The second type of relationship anxiety occurs more gradually and may have even been present in the very early stages of the relationship. This type of anxiety is characterized by a pervasive feeling of doubt, lack of attraction, the sense that you're really "just friends," and you're only staying in the relationship because you're too scared to be alone. Statements like, "We don't have enough chemistry" and "I'm settling" tend to dominate this type of relationship anxiety. This can be particularly disconcerting because, in a culture that exalts the in-love feelings as the sole indicator that you're with the "right" partner, the lack of those feelings in the beginning stages can easily spell doubt and doom (until you learn better). I often receive emails from people asking me if my work applies even if they had doubt from the beginning. The answer is yes. Anxiety is anxiety; it doesn't matter when or where it hits or even how it began. What matters is how you address it once it's here.

In either case—and if your anxiety falls somewhere between these two examples, this applies to you as well; remember that the ego is perpetually attempting to convince you that you're an exception—living with relationship anxiety often plummets people into what is referred to as the dark night of the soul. This is when everything familiar falls away, and you're invited—or dragged—to let go of aspects of yourself that aren't serving you, die several deaths, and eventually emerge into a new, more compassionate, wiser version of yourself. As with all the ways that anxiety manifests, you can resist the call and numb the pain, or you can walk through the center of the fear-storm and surrender to the most transformational ride of your life.

What Is Healthy Love?

In order to leave where we are, we need to know where we're going, and since our culture leaves us bereft of the principles, definitions, and actions that define healthy love, we must start here. As we've learned, anxiety is fueled by unrealistic expectations and faulty beliefs, and nowhere does that show up more than in the area of romantic love. It's time to update our cultural operating system and download new principles of healthy love so that we can attend to the realm of thoughts by replacing faulty beliefs with the truth.

The best place to start our updating process is, once again, with Jungian analyst Robert Johnson, who says, quite simply, that good love is like a bowl of oatmeal. A bowl of oatmeal? How unromantic, you may say. How prosaic, you think. Love should be an ice-cream sundae with cherries and sprinkles on top. Love should be a decadent Italian dessert. Oatmeal? How depressing.

In our romance-addicted culture, this concept rubs many people the wrong way and often elicits questions like: "Where's the passion, the drama, the excitement? Isn't love supposed to make me feel alive? Isn't it supposed to fulfill my every need, even needs I didn't know I had?"

What Johnson means is that love is *not* the cure-all that we set people up to believe it is. When love is true and real, it feels warm and sweet in your soul, the way oatmeal feels warm and nourishing in your belly. It feels good. It's not over-the-top, heart-stopping romance—the stuff Hollywood is made of. It just works. It's nice. It's comforting. And it might not work all the time, but for the most part, the two of you connect and click in a special way. And, because this doesn't happen every day, this is something to appreciate and celebrate.

Many people encounter problems in their relationships because the reality falls terribly short of their expectations. Because of a culturally induced brainwashing that creates a set of unrealistic and fantasy-based expectations, many people expect love to look and feel a certain way and are painfully plagued by a mental list of shoulds: "I *should* feel in love all the time. I *should* want sex all the time (or at least two to three times a week). I *should* look as happy as all my friends look on Facebook. I *should* always want to see my partner. I *should* always feel attracted. I *should* never feel irritated. I *should* feel sparkly like the sprinkles on top of my ice-cream sundae." But ask any couple married over twenty years, and they'll tell you that the sprinkles are not what you base a marriage on. They may shimmer in your daily life as a result of a sweet kiss or a satisfying conversation, but they're not the foundation of a marriage. These couples know what love is, and they know what it isn't. They know that love is not . . .

- **infatuation.** A relationship may begin as a feeling in a burst of excitement and passion, butterflies and fireworks, but this isn't real love—and it may not start this way, which doesn't render the relationship any less worthy or viable. Eventually the flames die down, and the process of learning about real loving begins.

- **an answer to your problems or the missing piece of your puzzle.** The only person who can rescue you from your challenges is you. The only person who can create your sense of aliveness and wholeness is you.

- **fitting into an image from romantic comedy or *People* magazine.**

- **unwavering certainty that you've met "the one."**

- **scintillating conversation every time you see each other.**

- **feeling attracted to your partner every moment of every day.**

- **effortless.**

- **liking each other all the time.** Your partner will irritate you to no end. That's normal.

Now let's explore what love is.
Love is . . .

- **action.** When you truly love someone, you learn what their love language is and make efforts as often as possible to express your love in the language that your partner can receive. For example, if your partner's love language is physical touch, you can say "I love you" all day long, but nothing will communicate your love as effectively as giving your partner a hug, a shoulder massage, or a kiss.

- **a choice.** We choose to take the risk of loving. We choose to practice opening our whole heart to our committed partner. We choose to break down the fear-barriers that try to convince us to run. We choose to challenge the false beliefs and unrealistic expectations propagated by popular culture, which says that you must be 100 percent certain that you're with the "right" person, "the one," your soulmate. We choose to commit and, through the commitment, allow ourselves to unfold into a lifetime of learning about love.

- **effort.** Real love will ask you to extend yourself for your partner in ways that stretch you beyond your comfort zone.

- **an opportunity to grow and learn about yourself.** Love asks you to extend yourself for the sake of the other. Love invites you to open your heart even when your habitual response is to shut down or withdraw in fear. Love pushes you to your edge, and on the projection screen of your partner's face, where every fear, insecurity, and old wound will be reflected, you will be asked to take full responsibility for your pain. Through the willingness to feel this pain, your heart will open to the joy of loving.

- **a risk.** Love says, "Risk everything that you are. Risk everything that you've known. Risk the safety and familiarity of your safe life." Because when you choose to say yes to love, you render your heart vulnerable to the risk of being hurt. Most of us construct elaborate defenses as a way to avoid taking this risk, even going so far as convincing ourselves that we must walk away from a loving, wonderful, honest relationship when the truth is that we're too scared to take the risk of loving.

- **more complicated than our culture dares to acknowledge, as evidenced by the fact that we only have one word for love.**

In *The Fisher King and the Handless Maiden*, Johnson writes:

> Sanskrit has ninety-six words for love; ancient Persian has eighty, Greek three, and English only one. This is indicative of the poverty of awareness or emphasis that we give to that tremendously important realm of feeling. Eskimos have thirty words for snow, because it is a life-and-death matter to them to have exact information about the element they live with so intimately. If we had a vocabulary of thirty words for love . . . we would immediately be richer and more intelligent in this human element so close to our heart. An Eskimo probably would die of clumsiness if he had only one word for snow; we are close to dying of loneliness because we have only one word for love. Of all the Western languages, English may be the most lacking when it comes to feeling.

There are so many ways to experience love. Yet when it comes to our intimate partners, we expect to feel *one* kind of love in *one* measurement: namely, "madly in love" without a hint of doubt or uncertainty clouding the pure, ecstatic experience. We exert immense and unrealistic levels of pressure on ourselves—especially during the early stages—to *feel* an exact amount and sentiment of love for our intimate partners. We believe that we can measure love, that there's a right way to love or an adequate quantity of love that signals that you've met the "right" partner and now you're legitimized to marry.

In order to widen our perspective on romantic love, it's helpful to break down the phrase "I love you" so that we start to see its variance and the multiplicity of ways to love your partner.

There's the *appreciation* you feel when he does something
thoughtful and kind, like brush the snow off your car in
twenty-degree weather or buy your favorite kind of bread.

There's the *comfort* you feel when you come home at the end
of a hard day at work, and she's there, waiting for you with
a plate of hot food and your favorite TV show cued up.

There's the *gratitude* you feel when she attends
the twelfth family gathering of the year.

There's the *warmth* you feel when you see him
across the room and know that he's your guy.

There are the *tingles* you feel when she kisses
you, maybe not every time, but enough to
know that a spark still burns between you.

There's the *trust* you feel when you walk
through a difficult conflict together and emerge
stronger than ever on the other side.

There's the *awe* you feel when you remember how rare it
is to find someone who "gets" you and whom you "get."

There's the *softness* you feel when you focus on
one physical quality in your partner that melts
your heart and brings a smile to your face.

There's the *joy* you feel when you listen to your favorite
song together or have a blast on the dance floor.

There's the *contentment* you feel when you read
together yet separately, before going to bed.

There's the feeling of *stability* that grows when you nurture the garden of your relationship year after year, enduring challenges and celebrating joys, and always knowing that you support your own and each other's growth and happiness.

When we attune our awareness and widen our consciousness to include these variations in our narrow cultural definition, we know that romantic love is multicolored and multidimensional. It's infinitely richer than the images presented on the big screen, infinitely more nuanced and alive than the one-dimensional feeling of butterflies that sometimes initiates a relationship. It's real and honest, and when we commit to loving one person with whom we can learn, it becomes one of the most fulfilling and meaningful paths we can embark upon.

Fear Eyes or Clear Eyes:
Love Is Not the Absence of Fear

As we continue to both widen and fine-tune our definition of love, we must recognize how deeply love and fear are intertwined. The failure to include fear in our understanding and expectations around love is one of our culture's biggest oversights and leads people toward untold amounts of anxiety. Just as grief and joy live in the same chamber of the heart, so love and fear are polarities designed to help us grow our capacity for loving. Fear is not our enemy, but if we don't know how to work with it when it arises in relationships, it can quickly fester and cause people to walk away from loving, available, well-matched partners. We must understand and respect fear's role so that it doesn't take over and morph into anxiety.

When we love another deeply, fear will rear its head. Designed to protect the vulnerable heart, fear is the sentry that guards the sacred entrances. The way past fear is not to engage in battle; that's a war you'll never win. The way to enter into love's passageways is to call fear by name. As we learned earlier in this book, we all need to be seen and heard, and fear is no exception.

When we call fear by name, we befriend it. And when we befriend it, it's no longer the enemy, something to be avoided or conquered. Befriending fear means making room for all of fear's manifestations: doubt, disconnection, uncertainty, lack of attraction, irritation, lack of the feeling of love, fantasizing about the perfect partner or an ex. These are the ways we know our heart is closed. When we buy into the belief that real love doesn't include these manifestations of fear, we believe that something is wrong when these feelings arise. Nothing is wrong. These states of being are all part of love. When we widen our definition of love—literally expanding it out like a giant balloon to include these more uncomfortable and certainly less glamorous feelings (not what we culturally associate with romantic love)—we feel our heart expanding as well.

Befriending how fear shows up in love means getting to know it, just like you would get to know a friend. When you befriend fear, you learn that sometimes fear is a wall; other times it's a curtain; still other times it's a layer of silt across the soul. From the mindset of curious exploration, you learn that your inner world is not a stark and defined place, as the ego would like to believe. It does not comprise sharp lines and definite answers that, once established, exist across time and space. The inner world is a mercurial, watercolor landscape where fear and love blend and collide and ultimately stand face-to-face so love can embrace fear in her soft wings.

When we deny fear, we perceive our partner and the world around us through fear eyes. Fear distorts perception. Or, rather, the denial of fear distorts perception. When we deny fear and banish it from our table, we see through eyes of lack: not enough love, not enough attraction, not enough humor, not enough conversation. There is no loveliness, no softness, no quality of allowing. It's the ego's world of harsh lines and its need for unilateral certainty. But when the wall or curtain rises up and you can say, "I'm feeling on edge. It's not you," the naming and the owning allow the barrier to melt.

And then a rush of essence. You see through clear eyes again. Your own essence appears like the river reeds in spring, and you see your lover as beauty on the banks. You see the intrinsic, unchangeable qualities of essence. You see his warmth and kindness flowing like a clear river. You see her honesty and humor unfold and bloom before your eyes, as if for the first time. It's first love all over again, or perhaps for the first time.

It would be so nice to remain in this open-eyed, open-hearted state always; but then we wouldn't be human. Being human includes closing up and shutting down. It includes retreat and withdrawal. Being human is almost defined by our separateness, as opposed to the oneness that apparently defines another realm. As separate human beings, we will disconnect; and as deeply thinking people prone to anxiety, doubt will invariably sidle onto the scene.

The culture has a very clear message about doubt: doubt means don't. If you experience any doubt about your partner, you're with the wrong partner. Any valid questioning and expression of healthy fears about your relationship are immediately interpreted as signs of a mistake.

For the anxious mind, doubt is inevitable. For the mind that examines every decision under the highest-resolution microscope possible, that asks important questions like, "How do I know that I love him? What is real love anyway? How do I know that we're not going to end up like my parents or as part of the 50 percent divorce statistic?" doubt is not only responsible, but is also another word for fear. And since fear's entire mission in life is to keep you protected from the possibility of getting hurt, it will naturally make a strong case in your most intimate relationship where the risk of pain is at its greatest. That's when fear—or doubt—shows up and tries to get you to run for the hills.

Should you listen? The answer lies in the wise words of one of my clients speaking about every area of her life (not just her relationship): "If I listened to doubt, I would never get out of bed in the morning." In other words, doubt is a normal part of the terrain of the anxious mind. When you learn to deal with anxiety effectively, you hear fear's lines, but you don't heed its advice; it will always shoot its darts into your mind, but you learn not to take the poison. To buy into the cultural lie that "doubt means don't" is like laying yourself prostrate at fear's feet and saying, "You win. You rule my life." And, as my client said, you would never get out of bed. You would live without risk in the safety of a carefully controlled box. You would be alive, but you wouldn't really be living. Working with anxiety means consciously stepping outside of that safe box, and romantic relationships offer us one of the most potent—and scary—places to practice this wholehearted risk taking.

Key Concepts for Understanding Relationship Anxiety: Projection and the Pursuer-Distancer Syndrome

In order to call fear to the mat, you need to be able to name fear's tricky ways of trying to convince you that you're with the wrong person and your anxiety is your intuition telling you to run. Our rate of relationship satisfaction would undoubtedly increase if everyone in an intimate relationship understood a couple of key concepts.

The first is projection. Projection is a defense mechanism where a person denies their own negative qualities or feelings and instead assigns them to someone else. In the context of intimate relationships, projection can occur in a variety of ways. If your husband had a very controlling mother, for example, he might *feel* controlled by your request that he drive more slowly, even if you're not being controlling. We would say then that he's projecting his mother onto you. Likewise, your wife might experience your need for sex as smothering because she hasn't attended to her invasion issues from a past relationship. We would say that she's projecting her ex onto you. This is when unconscious material that hasn't been fully processed creeps up into the relationship. If you've oriented your compass toward learning, you would trust that your partner isn't in fact being controlling or invasive, and would see it as an opportunity to heal an inner wound that needs attention.

Projection can also arise in the form of relationship anxiety when thoughts like, "I don't love him" or "I'm not in love with her" creep up. If you have a healthy relationship, and there's a core of connection—when anxiety isn't in the way—this is likely your fear projected onto your partner. The work then—and it can be very tough work because that voice sounds so convincing—is to pull the projection off your partner and address the core feelings inside you that need attention.

Sometimes this arises even several years into a marriage around a particularly painful transition. Let's say that your wife loses her father, to whom she was extremely close. If your wife is someone who has a hard time turning to face her painful feelings, she might deny her grief and loneliness, and then find that she's suddenly not feeling love for you anymore. Her squashed-down, painful feelings morphed into a projection onto you, because the ego-mind would prefer to focus on the tangible realm of thoughts rather than the vulnerable and amorphous realm of feelings. Her work then would be to pull the projection off you and find the willingness and courage to feel her pain.

If you hear the following thoughts spring up from nowhere, you're likely projecting.

- I don't love him or her anymore.

- I don't want this.

- We're too different.

- I always imagined myself with someone
  more [attractive, financially stable, educated,
  social, witty, sexual, affectionate, etc.].

Another way to understand projection is to think of it exactly as the word sounds: it's what's hidden or unconscious inside of you *projected* onto the screen of your partner. Your partner's face has become the movie screen. Your partner's mannerisms or laugh or the way he chews or lack of social fluidity can all become screens onto which your fears or difficult feelings are projected. If you're new to the concept of projection, it can be difficult to believe or understand. But if you roll it around in your mind for a while, you'll start to see that there's something here, and it will help you take responsibility for some of the shadow places inside you.

The second key concept to understand is the pursuer-distancer syndrome, a pattern in relationships that we've been brainwashed to believe is real love.

In almost every relationship there's a pursuer and a distancer. The pursuer is the one who holds the certainty, the in-love feelings, and the apparent lack of fear. The distancer is the one who carries the doubt, the lack-of-love feelings, and is more often the one erecting walls and barriers of various kinds. When a client says, "I was so in love with my last partner. I didn't have any doubt at all," I immediately ask, "Were you the pursuer or the distancer?" To which they invariably respond, "The pursuer. My partner was never fully available, and I always had the sense that there was one foot out the door." There's usually a thoughtful pause, and then, "The only time I've experienced butterflies and certainty is when my partner wasn't fully available. Once the chase ended, and I knew that he/she wasn't going anywhere, the walls went up and the doubt set in."

Many Hollywood films are predicated on the theme that the story ends when the relationship begins. This means that for ninety minutes, we're hooked on characters who are chasing after each other, always missing each other, both literally and emotionally. Our longing builds in direct proportion to their longing: watching them miss and then kiss and then miss each other again until—ah, at last!—they make mad, passionate love, and then ride off into the proverbial sunset.

As a result of this programming, we're wired to equate love with longing, which means that the only time we feel in love and certain is when our partner isn't fully available. We chase. We long. And then we think we're in love.

News flash: love is *not* longing.

It's essential to understand that it's not that the pursuer is more in love or has any less fear about intimacy than the distancer; rather, it's that the pursuer feels safer to let in the love feelings because he knows that his partner will put up a wall. This wall, no matter how subtle, makes it safe to feel "madly in love." If the tables were turned, and the distancer became the pursuer, as often happens at various points in a long-term relationship, the pursuer would then come into contact with his fears.

In *We: Understanding the Psychology of Romantic Love*, Robert Johnson writes:

> So much of our lives is spent in a longing and a search—for
> what, we do not know. So many of our ostensible "goals,"
> so many of the things we think we want, turn out to be the
> masks behind which our real desires hide; they are symbols
> for the actual values and qualities for which we hunger.
> They are not reducible to physical or material things, not
> even to a physical person; they are psychological qualities:

love, truth, honesty, loyalty, purpose—something we can feel is noble, precious, and worthy of our devotion. We try to reduce all this to something physical—a house, a car, a better job, or a human being—but it doesn't work. Without realizing it, we are searching for the *sacred*. And the sacred is not reducible to anything else.

Our culture misdirects the basic and essential human longing for the sacred onto people and things, primarily love relationships. So what happens when you find yourself with someone who's fully available and there's no longing? Or if you fall madly in love only to find the feelings fade or disappear one day? Or if those intense feelings of passion were never there to begin with? What typically happens is that you mistakenly assume that you're with the wrong person, that you don't really love them, or love them "enough." And if you're prone to anxiety or are an overthinker—and you don't understand the normal, healthy trajectory of love and concepts like projection—you'll likely find yourself spinning on the hamster wheel of anxiety, asking unanswerable questions.

Unlike the Hollywood version, that's when the work of learning about real love begins.

PRACTICE WORKING WITH PROJECTION

When you notice that you're stuck in your head or trapped in a projection, remember to call the witch by its true name and say, "I'm in a projection." That one simple act will help you de-fuse from the story that your fear-based mind is feeding you, and help you to take the next step, which is to ask, "What are these thoughts protecting me from feeling?" Then see if you can gently, with your inner wise parent at the helm, walk yourself through the process described in chapter 11, "Becoming

Curious about Longing," with the following subtle changes: Focus on your breath. Notice what you're feeling. Name any old patterns, beliefs, or stories that arise. Come back to the feelings. Above all, be gentle and have patience. None of this is fast or easy. But with time, commitment, and courage, you will start to notice the small shifts that lead to change.

NOTE »

*If you don't have children,
I encourage you to read this section
anyway and replace the focus on actual
children with your inner child. Also,
consider how your own upbringing
was different from or similar to the
principles revealed in this chapter and
the effect that they had on your anxiety.*

16

PARENTING IN AN
AGE OF ANXIETY

> There is no growth without real feeling. Children
> not loved for who they are do not learn how to love
> themselves. Their growth is an exercise in pleasing
> others, not in expanding through experience. As adults,
> they must learn to nurture their own lost child.
>
> MARION WOODMAN
> *Coming Home to Myself: Reflections for Nurturing
> a Woman's Body and Soul*

Our culture sets up an impossible model for parenting, one that is becoming more and more focused on perfection. And, as you've learned throughout the book, there are few things that create more anxiety than unrealistic expectations. Countless mothers have shared with me over the years that they feel like they're constantly doing something wrong no matter what area of parenting is being discussed: sleep, food, socializing, academics. Everywhere they look, they receive the message that their choices fall short of an impossible, unstated standard. As you now know, as soon as you're in the shame mindset of, "What's wrong with me?" it's a quick and slippery slope down the rabbit hole of anxiety.

The truth is that there is no manual for raising children, because no two children are the same and no parent-child configuration is the same. However, there are some basic premises that, when implemented, can make the challenging road of parenting a bit easier by calming some of the inherent anxiety that is par for the course. In this chapter, I will offer these premises and, by sharing stories of my own parenting journey and those of my clients, provide you a broad roadmap for what it looks like to parent with self-compassion and kindness, so we can raise children who know themselves, like themselves, and trust themselves. Ultimately, that's all we really want for our kids.

Worry Is the Work of Parenthood

Anxiety is part of parenting. It's not possible to care as deeply as we do about our children and not worry about them, and if we're judging ourselves for worrying, we only entrench the worry further. So before we launch into a wider discussion about parenting, we must make room for worry at the banquet table of the parenting psyche.

With each new baby, the worry makes an appearance all over again. If worry is in your genetic line, it will reappear during each transition as an opportunity to help you heal one more layer of this inherited trait. As always with transitions, when an unwanted trait rears its head, you can either learn how to work with it, which leads to growth, or ignore it, which causes it to become even further embedded into your psychological makeup. Most people, without consciousness and guidance around transitions, take the path of least resistance and allow the habit to become further ingrained. Parenting offers daily opportunities to learn to work with worry more consciously and effectively.

This point was driven home when I was giving birth to my second son. I was twelve hours into my labor but hadn't progressed into the strong contractions that would push my baby into the world. My midwife could sense that something was emotionally holding me back from the internal surrender that needed to occur before my body would open enough to move to the next stage of labor. She moved closer to me and said, "You look so sad." And that's when the floodgates opened, and I cried about how worried I was over losing my exclusive relationship with Everest, how worried I was about how Everest would respond to his little brother, how worried I was about my ability to love another child the way I loved Everest. She sat at the bottom of my bed and said to me, "Worry is the work of motherhood," quoting from Pam England's book *Birthing from Within*.

I had come across that sentence when I read the book during my first pregnancy, but there was no way for me to metabolize what it meant until I became a mother. When Everest was a baby, I worried constantly about him: Was he healthy? Was he happy? Would he get hurt? Was he hungry? Was he in pain? When my husband would take him for a few hours, I could barely relax from the worry about their safety. I would have catastrophic visions of car accidents and police officers appearing at my door. I felt grateful for the invention of the cell phone and utilized it multiple times during each of their excursions. *Worry is the work of motherhood.*

As Everest got older, I worried less. He was more stable, less vulnerable, years away from the baby and toddler stages when I would check to make sure he was still breathing at night, every night, usually several times a night. My husband could take him for a day, and I usually wouldn't need a cell phone check in (although I didn't oppose a text message). I developed more trust that Everest was going to be okay, and that if he wasn't okay (if he got hurt or sick), I would find the resources to handle it. I became more adept at utilizing the following keys to manage the inherent worry of parenting.

The first key, as I mentioned, is to accept that worry is part of parenthood. We've talked extensively about accepting and embracing the authentic and existential feelings of grief, fear, jealousy, boredom, and loneliness, which are part of being human. We don't usually include worry on this list, but when it comes to parenting, it's nearly impossible to love a child as deeply as we do without worrying about their well-being. Context invites acceptance, which inspires compassion; when we accept the worry instead of judging or berating ourselves for carrying it, it becomes easier to manage.

The second key is to accept your powerlessness over the outcome of your children's lives, including their day-to-day health and their long-term emotional well-being. Of course, we do everything in our power to make sure they're healthy and safe, but since we can't put them in a bubble, we have to accept that life will happen. Bee stings will occur, bones will break, illness and fevers will take over, accidents will happen. This is a continual lesson in surrendering control: reminding ourselves every day, usually several times a day, that we cannot control most of what occurs in our kids' lives. Our egos just hate that reality! But our higher selves take solace in that fact because it means that we can only do what we can do, and the rest is in higher hands.

The third key is to pray. Every night since my kids were born, I've prayed to God to please keep them safe, to please keep my husband and me safe, to help me be the best mother I can be. When I used to see Everest climbing up to a high spot on a play structure, I prayed. When he was sick, I prayed. When I saw Asher struggling with the immense discomfort of new teeth trying to pierce through bones and gums, I prayed. And when the worry threatened to consume me to the point where it eclipsed my joy, I prayed. "Dear God, please remove my worry. Please help me surrender. Please help me." As I've said at other points in this book, even if you don't believe in prayer, pray anyway. It helps to move the energy along some invisible channels that you don't have to believe in for them to do their work.

The fourth key is to practice gratitude. Worry is a negative frequency, the mind's habitual tendency to focus on something bad happening. When my boys were young, I practiced daily visualizing changing the channel on my internal television set from worry to gratitude until it became a habit. On the worry screen, I would see Everest falling down the stairs or tumbling off a play structure (horrible images). But when I changed the channel, I tuned into the gratitude station. And there, projected on the screen, I would see my beautiful, healthy, happy sons. I would see their shining faces and big smiles. I would see Everest running across our green grass, laughing his head off as he tried to avoid the sprinklers. I would see Asher, safely tucked into the sling, watching his big brother like he was watching a hero, a big, toothless grin spreading across his face, brighter than the sun. Sometimes I would see them as young men, standing with their arms around each other, leaning against our fence, laughing at some inside joke as my husband and I took their picture. Sometimes I would see even beyond that, to wedding days and other joyous occasions. And then I would come back to the now, this moment, and the sheer joy of watching them as they moved through the day.

Three Antianxiety Medications for Parents: Gratitude, Attunement, Taking the Long View

Let's talk a bit more about gratitude as it's such a powerful antidote to anxiety. If a parent is disconnected from gratitude, the joy and excitement of raising a child quickly degenerates into resentment and a sense of drudgery. Among many other things, parenthood is a sacrifice, and, for women, the sacrifice begins during pregnancy. A woman hands over her body to house the growth of a new human being; she births the baby during the ultimate initiation of her life; and then she must lovingly care for the child day and night, sacrificing sleep, freedom, separateness, and sexuality to varying degrees for various lengths of time so the child survives, thrives, and hopefully grows into a caring, compassionate, confident adult. What a task! And none of it would be worth it if we failed to see the miracle inherent to every stage of this process.

One of the misconceptions about gratitude is the belief that you have to feel it in order to connect to it. You don't. Sometimes gratitude washes over us like water, and the feeling floods you like warm sun on a cold winter's day. But more often than not, especially knee-deep in the often overwhelming, usually exhausting years of raising children, gratitude is something that you must reach toward until, like a steady hand, it reaches back to you. Just like smiling even when you're not happy can bring a moment of calm to your nervous system, saying thank you even if you don't feel grateful can help you tap into and activate the current of gratitude inside of you.

We do this by remembering to slow down and say, out loud, thank you. We do this by looking with eyes that see and hearing with ears that listen. One of the many reasons why my husband and I loved co-sleeping for so many years is that it was built-in time of lying down next to our kids and seeing all the day's stresses and frustrations unravel and float away until only the soft, angelic face of sleep was left.

And the two words that naturally emerged from my lips every night as I stared in awe at their peaceful beauty were: *thank you*.

If you have a child entrusted into your care, you are blessed, indeed. When you take the time to acknowledge the blessing, the normal negativity in the day in the life of a modern parent is absorbed into the positive stream of love and gratitude that can fuel your days.

The second antianxiety medication for parents is to learn to attune to who your child is, not who you wish she would be. At some point, every mother and father have to grieve their fantasy child so that they can embrace the child they have. You thought your child would excel at sports, and it turns out she's a bookworm. You thought he would follow in your footsteps and love science, but he's in love with music. We have ideas of who we think our children will be, and those ideas need to shatter and be grieved, otherwise they will mutate into anxiety. You grieve so that you can see accurately and love fully, thereby supporting who your child is, not who you wish he would be. Just like anxiety is created when you try to contort yourself into the mold that our culture says you should be in, when we do this with our children, we're perpetuating this damaging cycle, not only calling up our own anxiety but also transmitting it down to our children with the message that they're wrong in some way.

When you listen and attune closely, you'll remember that what you want most for your children—above any superficial achievement—is to be fulfilled. When you can step out of the culture's obsession with achievement and perfection and instead step into the commitment of seeing your children for who they actually are, you'll quickly notice their unique spark, their wiring, their way of moving through the world.

In my opinion, one of the primary tasks of parenting is to mirror back and support your child's interests, to notice what lights them up, and then pour energy into supporting that spark, whatever it is. When I'm working with new parents, I encourage them to "watch for the spark," to pay close attention to those activities that capture their child's attention and imagination. And I have no doubt that every single child has places or activities or books or people or subjects that light them up.

For example, I'm amazed when I look at pictures from my older son's first two years of life and see him doing things like opening and shutting the zipper on a suitcase to figure out how it worked. His engineering mind appeared by age one and was fully apparent at eighteen months old. And I'm fascinated by how different our second son's interests are, which also showed themselves early in life.

If you watch closely, you will see your child's spark. The key is to get your own agenda out of the way so that you can clearly see what's before you. If you have a desire for your daughter to be a dancer, but she clearly shows interest in science, you may miss the science clues altogether if your vision is clouded by your own desires. It's a powerful psychological truth that children live out the unlived lives of their parents on many levels, so we must do our best to carefully attend to our own latent desires so that we don't impose those on our kids. Sometimes just naming it helps move it from the unconscious realm to the conscious. By saying aloud, "You know, I feel so sad that I didn't pursue my passion for dance," you can own it and, by doing so, free your child to live their own life.

The third antianxiety medication for parents is to focus on the long view. Parenting is a long road, yet it's easy to become caught up in the immediate anxieties that are consuming you. When your baby resists the car seat and treats it like a torture chamber, it can be helpful to look at older children and realize that all kids learn to tolerate being in the car. When your toddler struggles with potty training, it can be helpful to remember that everyone eventually learns to use the toilet; you won't have a middle schooler in diapers! I can't tell you how many times I've been anxious about my kids doing or not doing something, only to realize a few months later that that particular issue has passed.

Taking the long view alleviates anxiety that stems from a culture that tells you that everything has to happen on a particular timeline. When you shuck off this arbitrary timeline, waves of spaciousness open up inside of you, which in turn reverberate positively to your child. Yet in our culture, which pushes comparisons and expectations of success at every turn, this is easier said than done.

The race to achieve and succeed begins early. From learning to sit up, crawl, walk, and talk, the first two years are defined by developmental milestones. We may not consciously subscribe to the cultural race to be the biggest, fastest, smartest, and best, but when your baby doesn't walk until sixteen months or talk until two (or later), it's difficult not to fall prey to the insidious belief that something's wrong, followed by the more insidious anxiety that ensues. Conversely, when your baby crawls at seven months and is saying their first words before their first birthday, it's difficult not to secretly ascribe significance to these developments and assume they mean that your baby is more intelligent than others in their age group.

The truth is that none of those milestones have any correlation to intelligence, and when we buy into this story, we easily fall into the pit of anxiety. From talking to learning how to swim and read, weaning to sleeping through the night, we rush and sometimes push our babies and children to learn and compete, often before they're ready. A child-led parenting style means watching and listening to your child's cues while sensitively, in conjunction with your own needs as a parent, allowing the child to determine the timing of as many events as possible. Again, when you can step out of the cultural expectations regarding what's "normal" and instead listen to and trust your child's rhythm, your anxiety will decrease.

The story that always comes to mind when I'm talking about timelines and rhythm is about my older son learning to swim. I took him to swimming lessons every summer from the time he was four through six, but he usually lasted one lesson, and then would look at me and say, "Mommy, I told you I'm going to teach myself to swim." Still, I persisted, and still he resisted and insisted that he would teach himself. Sure enough, his first time in the pool the summer he turned nine, he dove underwater and emerged with an ecstatic grin on his face, then proceeded to swim beautifully across the pool. "I told you, Mommy!" It was a celebratory day for everyone.

Along these lines, I'll never forget when my well-meaning neighbor observed my seven-year-old boy riding his bike with training wheels and said, "He's still not riding on two wheels?" His kids, several years younger, had been riding a bike for many years. I can't even recall when my oldest learned to ride a bike, but what I do know is that it was a joyous moment determined by his own readiness. What does it really matter if a child learns to ride a two-wheeler at age four, seven, or nine?

Weaning, swimming, riding a bike, learning to read. What's the rush? Why do we culturally transmit a belief that earlier is better? And the race seems to be running at increasingly higher levels of pressure and intensity. When I was a child, it wasn't uncommon for kids to learn to swim or ride a bike at the later end of single-digit ages without receiving any social stigma or pressure. Now, if your child isn't reading, swimming, and riding a bike by the time they leave kindergarten, you all run the risk of being judged. It's time to slow the pace back down, for our own sake and the sake of kids. When we slow everything down, anxiety takes a breath, and we're better able to come back into ourselves where our wisdom and clarity live. Every time we practice stepping out of societal expectations and trusting ourselves not only do we take a bite out of anxiety, but we also model self-trust for our kids, which is one of the greatest gifts we can give them.

Helping Children with Anxiety

Most of the books on kids and anxiety (and there are dozens since anxiety in young people is on the rise) focus on cognitive-behavioral therapy (CBT) methods for working with anxiety. While I utilize and teach some CBT tools, I also take a different approach, one that seeks to reduce anxiety in children from the outset and help parents understand and meet the core needs when anxiety does arise, just as I do with adults. If we medicate anxiety away, we miss the message. Breathing tools are essential, but they don't meet anxiety at the root. You have to go deeper, which means helping your kids feel their feelings and making sure they know that they're fully loved exactly as they are.

Teaching Kids to Feel Their Feelings

One of the primary roles as a parent is to teach kids how to soften their hearts and allow themselves to feel their difficult feelings. When my kids were younger, I felt immensely overwhelmed by this task and longed for elders to teach my kids how to work effectively with their sensitivity and channel the big feelings toward creative and spiritual avenues instead of allowing them turn into anxiety. In the absence of guides and through trial and error, eventually I developed the following touchstones to help my kids navigate through the tumultuous and often terrifying feelings of being a small child in a big world, which often revolve around the fear of death.

Touchstones to Help Children Navigate Their Feelings

Whenever you see that your child's pain is causing anxiety, remind him to practice Tonglen, the simple practice of breathing in the pain and breathing out a prayer of love. For example, if he hears sad news, and you see your child rubbing his eyes or trying to stop or control the loss in some way, say, "What can you do when you feel loss?" With enough reminders, your child will incorporate the practice and develop a habit of moving toward the pain instead of away from it. And when I say "enough reminders," I mean thousands and thousands. Just like with adults, there are no quick fixes for moving through pain and working with anxiety.

Spend time every night talking about what made your child feel sad that day. When my son was young, I would hold him on the bed while he unloaded the daily list, which often included snippets of conversations he may have overheard years before. Here's a sample list from when my older son was about seven years old.

- The raccoon I saw on the side of the road on our way to the science museum.

- That people die.

- That sometimes babies die before they come out of their mommies.

- A couple of years ago, I heard a neighbor
  tell you about a girl who drowned.

- That you and daddy are going to die one day.

When your child shares her fears, gently rest your hand on her heart and ask her to breathe into the pain. You can say something like, "There's a lot of pain this world, and there is also so much beauty. One of my jobs as your parent is to teach you that you can handle the pain, because you can. Pain is energy. It hurts to feel it, but it hurts more not to feel it. When you cry, the pain moves through you, and you cleanse your soul. So let's breathe into the pain, and then say a prayer for the raccoon and the parents of the girl who drowned." Then talk about all of the happy parts of the day. Here's another sample list.

- When Asher made me laugh.
- When I took care of Asher because his toe was hurting.
- The beautiful trees.
- The beautiful full moon.
- Throwing berries in the creek and catching them downstream.
- The bees. (He loves bees.)

As you can see from the first list, most of a child's fears ultimately boil down to a fear of death, which is extremely common for sensitive kids. When my son would express fear and sadness about me dying one day, I would say to him, "Everest, when it's my time to die, you'll be okay. You'll cry a lot, and it will hurt in your heart, but you'll be okay. Most likely, I'm not going to die for a long time, and you'll be a grown man with a partner and kids that you love more than anything in the world. Right now, you love me and Daddy and Asher more than anything, and it's hard for you to imagine that changing, but it will change. One day you'll love someone so much that you'll want to marry that person, just like Daddy wanted to marry me, and you'll have kids with that person. When I die, your partner will hold you when you cry. You might cry for many weeks, and you might grieve on and off for a year or longer, but you'll be okay." I don't want to set up false hope that I'll live into old age, but I do want to communicate the message that when I die, he'll find the comfort and resources to handle it.

Encourage your child to find their own tools for handling anxiety. One night when my older son was about eight years old, he was trying to fall asleep, and he said, "Mommy, I want to say a prayer for the dead moths that Asher finds." He then proceeded to whisper the most beautiful, heartfelt prayer I've ever heard. In its purity, it was like poetry whispered from the mouth of an angel. Then he wanted to say a prayer for the mice that our new neighbors had recently found, dead and decaying, in the walls of the house that they were renovating. Again, his entire being shifted into a higher frequency when he allowed the words to spontaneously be carried from his heart to his lips, like little lanterns of light. He finished with a big smile on his face and fell asleep more quickly than he had in months.

Create rituals to acknowledge and contain the loss and rebirth on the solstices and equinoxes. Using these transitional days in the calendar to practice letting go, you can enact rituals like writing down on leaves the things you want to let go of, then sending them down a creek or on the wind. Even simple rituals can help contain and soothe the fear of loss.

Laugh, dance, tickle, and hug as much as possible. Play and laughter are antidotes to anxiety.

I offer these tools and touchstones, but the truth is that we don't exactly know what works and what doesn't when it comes to raising children. What I can tell you is that by the time my older son became a teenager, he had no fear of death. I mean, zero. In fact, a few days after his fourteenth birthday, he soloed in a glider, literally flying into the sky by himself. The child who was afraid of everything grew into a young man who is afraid of almost nothing. It seemed impossible to imagine when he was younger, and still blows my mind when I think about it. This is what I mean by taking the long view: we simply have no idea how our child will grow and mature, but when we can trust and see a vision of them growing through some of their anxiety (with our loving attention) and leaving it behind, a chunk of our own anxiety about their well-being will be released.

Fully Loved

Perhaps one of the most powerful vaccinations against anxiety is to know you are fully loved. One way we can limit anxiety in kids—it might not be entirely preventable given the culture we live in—is to transmit that message daily. This is where your own process of self-reflection and inner work come in, for the more aware you are of your trigger points, the less reactive you'll be to your child's less-than-lovely yet totally normal behavior.

For example, if you haven't dealt with your own issues around worthiness and performance, you will pass on the inherited beliefs that your job as parents is to mold and shape behavior so that your child becomes a high-achieving, successful member of society. Parents are encouraged to do this by following the advice of a "good job" culture that praises behavior instead of essence, outcome over effort, gold stars and high grades over passion. When Mommy's face lights up when Billy draws a "perfect" tree but doesn't when he struggles with basketball, he will naturally direct his energy toward the place where he receives positive feedback. In other words, he may love basketball more than drawing, but Mommy seemed so impressed by his tree, that he pursues an area that isn't his passion.

Where this becomes especially damaging is in the realm of big feelings. Mommy smiles when Billy behaves well, which means not making too much noise, not crying, not showing anger, being agreeable and helpful, going to bed on time. She trains him to be a good boy and, in the process, runs the risk of annihilating his essential nature, which may be loud, boisterous, or sensitive. The message he receives is that he's only loved when he's good (normal, fits into the mold, agreeable, not too loud or messy).

As a parent, one of my deepest desires is for my sons to know that they are lovable and loved exactly as they are, no matter how angry, loud, messy, or disrespectful they are. I want them to know that all their feelings are welcome and important. I may not always like their behavior—and I let them know—but it doesn't alter my love for them, which is unchanging and eternal. I'll say to them, "I didn't like how you treated your friend today, but nothing will ever change how much

I love you." The message I hope to impart is: I love you because I love you. I don't love you because you're beautiful (even though you are). I don't love you because you're creative (although I do reflect back an awareness of your creativity). I love you because I love you. And that will never change no matter what you do.

PRACTICE SEEING YOURSELF THROUGH EYES OF LOVE

One of the great challenges of parenting is that we inevitably pass on our unhealed places to our kids, and we all have unhealed places, because we're all human. If we were meant to raise completely healthy people, there would have been a different plan in place, so it can be helpful to trust that when we're feeling anxious about messing up our kids, this is all part of the plan. In some way that we can't understand, we're supposed to mess up our kids in one way or another. When we remember this, a layer of anxiety is eased. It's not that we're giving ourselves permission to slack off, but if you're a parent reading this book, you're more the type of person to obsess about being a better parent than you are the type to slack off.

So as we near the end of this book, we come to another practice of self-love, for the more we love ourselves, the more we will naturally and effortlessly love our children. This is a practice for helping you connect to your essence.

1. Close your eyes and imagine the most loving person in the world sitting next to you. Perhaps this is a grandmother, living or deceased, who delights in the

sight of you, whose smile reflects her unconditional love. Perhaps it's an animal, a creature that knows you so well and loves you simply because you exist. Perhaps it's a friend or your partner who gets you completely and has no trouble reflecting back why he or she loves you. This person can be real or imagined, but the energy that they resonate is pure love and unconditional acceptance.

2. Now imagine that this person is looking into your eyes and can see directly into your soul. She or he wants to tell you what they see: the qualities that describe you; the strands of your being; who you are in your essence. There may or may not be words attached to this description, but through this communication, you receive a direct transmission of who you are and a clear awareness that you are loved because you exist. That you are worthy without having to prove anything. That you are good, enough, and good enough. That you are wholly and completely loved.

EPILOGUE

This is the beginning of a road whose end
is totally unknown and totally known.

MARION WOODMAN
Bone: Dying into Life

When I'm working with people struggling with anxiety, they often ask, "When will the anxiety end?" I tell them, "That's like asking when will my dehydration headaches end?" Just as headaches alert us to thirst, so anxiety alerts us to needs. If we eliminate the symptoms, how will we determine the needs? As you've learned throughout this book, anxiety is a messenger from the unconscious. It invites you to listen to your body, attend to your thoughts skillfully, meet your heart with tenderness, and water your soul. With the shift in mindset from seeing anxiety as a problem to seeing it as a gift, everything changes. Then, and only then, can you begin to harness its wisdom and, paradoxically, be released from its stronghold. When worked with effectively, anxiety transforms from an enemy to a friend, loosens its grip on your life, and becomes a portal to freedom.

As Rainer Maria Rilke said, "Be patient toward all that is unsolved in your heart, and love the questions themselves." When embarking on inner work, it's essential to remember that life is a work in progress, and there is no end goal to healing. As humans, we are both whole and broken, formed and unformed. But there is a critical difference between having broken parts that need attention and believing that there is something fundamentally wrong with you. *There is nothing wrong with you.* You are intrinsically good, loved, and whole. We all have plenty of defenses and wounds; they're a sign of being human. But we have so much more that's healthy and right. Your place of wholeness dwells undisturbed beneath the walls and wounds of your defenses and heartaches. You needed the walls to survive the pain of childhood, even the secondhand pain of absorbing the unattended wounds of loving parents, but you no longer need them. The healing work as adults is to soften the walls slowly and gently, with great love, until they crumble and fall to reveal the untouched garden of the true self.

Like a labyrinth, you follow the symptoms of anxiety as you spiral into the center point of self, then spiral back out again into the world, and back again into the center of self. Inward and outward, giving and receiving, in-breath and out-breath, filling the waters of the inner well until they overflow into the world, and touching the heart of the world as you continue your inward healing path. This is how we serve from a place of fullness instead of emptiness, from joy instead of obligation. The more our hearts open and soften, the more the hardened husks of protection and defense fall away. With an undefended heart, we're in direct contact with the pain of the world, and we are compelled to act, to give, and to serve.

This is the wisdom of anxiety: the call to turn inward so that you can fill your well and turn back outward to give to a world that needs you. The time is now.

ACKNOWLEDGMENTS

I'm deeply grateful to:

My teachers in the Jungian depth psychology tradition: Robert Johnson, Marion Woodman, Joseph Campbell, and of course, Carl Jung. I am a vessel of this lineage, and this book would not exist without their teachings. I am also indebted to the Buddhist teachings of Pema Chödrön, who has been a guide for decades.

I'm particularly grateful to Jungian analyst Robert Johnson for coming to me in a dream in April 2015 to tell me it was time to write another book. His words and wisdom are woven throughout these pages.

My clients, readers, and course members who have bravely allowed me to enter their inner worlds, where we walk together through the terrain of anxiety and learn to listen to its wisdom. You are my true teachers.

Carrie Dinow, Jessica Hicks, Lisa Dunn, Lisa Rappaport, Kariane Nemer, Nicol Pate, Sarah Peltzie. I am blessed to be surrounded by a circle of wise and loving sisters, and I would not be who I am without you.

Dr. Bruce Gregory, who guided me through my twenties, and Rabbi Dr. Tirzah Firestone, who is my guide for life.

My parents, Margaret Paul and Jordan Paul, who planted the love of learning and the seeds of psychological pursuit in me as a child. I have followed in your footsteps in so many ways, and I'm deeply grateful for everything you've modeled and taught me.

Haven Iverson at Sounds True. Thank you for your vision, your support, and for helping me weave the disparate squares of the first draft into a cohesive quilt.

My sons, Asher and Everest, radiant beings of light who have taught me everything I know about raising sensitive children. The privilege of being your mother is a gift beyond words.

My husband, Daev Finn, the foundational stone upon which our life of beauty rests, my safe cove inside of which I can bare my truest self, the one who teaches me every day about real love and real romance. As Shams was to Rumi, you are Friend in every sense of the word.

And to the mystery of the unconscious, what Gary Zukav calls Soul and what Carl Jung calls the Self. I bow down with humility to this abiding principle, which has dragged me into my own underworld, again and again, to wrestle with angels dark and light so that I could shed the habits, beliefs, mindsets, and actions that no longer served and, in doing so, can help others do the same.

APPENDIX A

RELATIONSHIP RED FLAGS

All my work on relationships and anxiety is predicated on the assumption that you're in a healthy, loving relationship without red flags. Relationship red flags are:

- emotional, physical, or sexual *abuse* currently occurring in the relationship;

- any *addiction*, which includes alcohol, drugs, gambling, sex, and in some cases work and media;

- unhealed issues around *trust* and betrayal;

- severe issues around *control*—keeping in mind that everyone has control issues, but what I'm talking about is deep control issues where one person feels consistently trapped or unsafe by the other's need for control;

- *irreconcilable differences around core values* like religion or having children—for example, one of you definitely wants to have kids and the other definitely doesn't.

Let me say here—because I've been doing this work for so long and I can hear when an anxious spike might arise—that having differences is *not* a red flag issue! Everyone has differences, and many couples have vast differences about things like how they like to spend their time. You're not meant to partner with your clone. Differences are to be expected and even valued. But I'm talking about core differ-ences where there is simply no way to compromise without one of you sacrificing a deeply held value.

If you can identify any of these issues in your relationship, I encour-age you both to seek support through counseling and/or twelve-step programs. I will also say that almost all red flag issues can be healed if both people are committed to the healing.

TWO WAYS TO JOURNAL

The following are basic guidelines for two types of journaling. These guidelines emerged from my work with clients and course members who sometimes agonize about doing journaling the "right" way or express fear about what they'll discover when they start to journal. Having simple guidelines can alleviate some of the natural anxiety that arises when we begin a new practice that seeks to excavate the hidden contents of our inner world.

Also, if the common fear arises that says, "I'm scared of what I'll find when I start to journal," keep in mind that from the thousands of people I've walked through this process, I see the same things arise: more clarity, more equanimity, more serenity, and of course, more love. It's a simple equation—less fear equals more love—and when you engage in a daily, committed practice like journaling, you will contain and reduce your fear, which will allow your self-love and your love for others to bloom.

Open-Ended Journaling

GUIDELINES FOR OPEN-ENDED JOURNALING

- Remind yourself before you start that there isn't a "right" way to journal. Set your intention to explore and learn and stay open. Be curious about your inner world. Talk to yourself the way you wish your parents would have talked to you. Make time to get to know yourself. Curiosity is the key. Try to let go of judgment, but if judgment arrives, become curious about that as well.

- Remind yourself that journaling is just for you, and it doesn't have to be perfect, pretty, brilliant, witty, or grammatically correct. Nobody will ever see it. It's not for publication, and it's not for a grade. It's only for you. Be as messy and imperfect as possible. Let it all hang out. Don't censor. Don't edit. Just express.

- Ask open-ended questions and trust the answers. Try not to overthink. Write before you have a chance to think too much about the answers. One way to do this is to keep your hand moving.

- If you're scared about what you might learn or discover when you start to journal, you're not alone. It takes courage to dive into uncharted waters, and if journaling is new for you it might feel particularly scary. You may feel resistance, and if that's the case, I suggest that you start by journaling with the fear and resistance itself. Remember that everything inside of us wants to be seen and heard. When you give attention to the fear and resistance, you will notice that it transforms.

- If you're concerned about someone else reading your journal, consider journaling on your computer and then deleting the files immediately. The record of the journaling isn't as important as having a space to unload and examine the contents of your inner world.

- If writing isn't your thing, you can also "journal" out loud by speaking into a recorder or simply speaking aloud in the shower or your car. What matters isn't the form the journaling takes but that you take time to unload what's churning inside of you.

- If you start to feel overwhelmed by your thoughts and feelings—as can happen in this open-ended or

stream-of-consciousness type of journaling—shift into
the guided journaling technique that I explain next.

QUESTIONS FOR OPEN-ENDED JOURNALING

- What do I love?
- What brings me joy?
- Whom do I enjoy spending time with?
- How do I feel about my relationship
  with my mother/father/siblings?
- What do I want for my life?
- What's my earliest memory?
- What's my most painful memory?
- How did my parents or caregivers respond to my pain?
- What are the beliefs I absorbed about pain?
- What's my happiest memory?
- What's my favorite place on earth?
- What do I value?
- What are my favorite foods?
- How do I feel about my body?
- Do I allow myself time to rest?
- What are my beliefs about rest?

Many people like to end their journaling sessions by making a gratitude list, especially if they found themselves in painful territory. It's
not about dismissing your pain but about being able to hold both the
pain and the gratitude simultaneously, which means feeling the pain
but also orienting toward gratitude.

Guided Journaling: Dialoguing
with the Different Parts of You

Dialoguing is a simple journaling technique to work with anxiety
when it arises, and it's the main tool I use with my clients and with
myself. It's a journaling technique where you will engage in a dialogue
between the different parts of you and learn to move toward them

with kindness. Like the stream-of-consciousness journaling, it can be done on paper or out loud, and all of the previous guidelines apply.

Some people do very well with open-ended journaling, but others feel flooded when they immerse themselves in the stream of consciousness without any rational—or left-brain, inner parent—part of them tempering the flood. In the language of the brain, when you're writing from your body and spending time in the feeling realm, you're activating the right hemisphere, the part that lives in the world of raw emotion, images, metaphors, and autobiographical memory. This is a beautiful world, but if you spend too much time there, especially if anxiety is activated, you may feel flooded, and the journaling can be counterproductive.

Before we dive into the technique, it's essential to have an overview of the parts of yourself, the different characters that are living inside of you at all times. We each have multiple parts that rear up during different situations. When you understand these parts, you can start to name them and create some separateness; then you decide if it's a part of you that needs more attention and, if so, what kind of attention.

In the center is the core Self. This is the essential you: the you that is solid and secure, confident and loving. This is the you that doesn't care about what other people think, that has a clear sense of purpose and direction, that is able to allow your feelings and thoughts to float through you without attaching onto them. This is the part of you that was born whole without having to prove yourself, that knows that you are worthy and lovable exactly as you are. This is the part of you that carries your intrinsic qualities: your gifts, your interests, your passions, your personality characteristics like kindness or a sense of humor—the part of you that is independent from the transitory nature of externals, like looks or salary.

Then you have the fear-based ego. This is the part of you that struggles with the transitory nature of being human, that clings to the way things are, resists change, believes that the world isn't safe and that others aren't safe, and is committed at all costs to preserving its illusion that it can control others and outcomes. Regardless of how loving our childhood was, we all have an ego self; it's just part of being human.

Lastly, we have our different masks or personas that develop as we grow up. Carl Jung understood that we all have parts of our personalities that are like different characters—or archetypes—living inside of us. The more we bring these characters to light—which means bringing them from the unconscious to the conscious—the more we can work with them, bring compassion to them, and make choices regarding how much power we give them.

Common characters include:

- the caretaker
- the protector
- the chameleon
- the jealous/envious one
- the good girl/good boy
- the bad girl/bad boy
- the judge
- the bully
- the taskmaster

A lot of these overlap, and most are adaptive and protective parts of you that grew from painful situations as a child. For example, if you grew up in a situation where you were abused or ridiculed every time you cried, a protector developed with a belief system that said, "It's not safe to cry. It's not safe to be me. I have to shut down parts of myself in order to survive."

When we start to move toward these adaptive parts of ourselves instead of trying to push them away or judge them, we learn that underneath them lives the soft, vulnerable core Self. Sometimes these parts can feel like an inner bully—like a judgmental part that is incessantly critical of everything you do—but when you soften into that part and even approach it with love, it starts to crumble and lose its grip. Inside every bully lives a scared child, and the same is true for the inner bullies. Journaling helps you engage with these different parts of you with curiosity and compassion—a mindset of learning—which helps you to de-fuse from them. Being fused with our wounded inner characters causes anxiety. When we journal, we develop our calm, inner adult who allows us to de-fuse.

Here's an example of a fictitious dialogue I wrote for a blog post called, "Am I Meant to Be with My Ex?" in which I explain that the first step in breaking free from this kind of rumination or intrusive thought is to name what's actually happening. It's a powerful first step, and when you can repeatedly name your experience with conviction, it's like casting a powerful spell that breaks the allure of the fantasy. Eckhart Tolle says that the ego thrives on control, which is really the illusion of control. Once you identify the ego's tactics, it begins to lose its power.

> **Ego.** "There you go, thinking about your ex again.
> You had such amazing chemistry, and you dream
> about him (her) at least once a week. That must
> mean that you're meant to be with him (or her)."

> **Self.** "I know that's what it feels like, but that's not
> actually true. It's an illusion of my mind, your way
> to distract me from the risk of the here and now, of
> opening my heart to my present, available partner. I'm
> not going to indulge those thoughts anymore."

> **Ego.** "That's crap. Just admit it: you're still in love with him.
> You'll never feel as excited about your partner as you did about
> your ex. Why do you keep feeding me these ridiculous lines?"

> **Self.** "It's you who's feeding the lines. It's you who can't let go.
> It's you who is trying to convince me that I don't really love
> my partner. I know you're scared. I know you don't want me
> to risk making myself vulnerable. I know that when I think
> about my ex, I feel safer in some way, sequestering myself in
> that same, familiar room in my mind. But I'm not going to do
> that anymore. Instead I want to know what you're afraid of."

Ego. "I told you: I'm not scared! I'm telling you the truth, and if you choose not to listen, you're going to settle for less than what you deserve."

Self. "You sound incredibly convincing, but every time I listen to you, I feel anxious and confused. Listening to you ramble about my ex isn't serving me. But if you want to tell me what you're scared of, I'm happy to listen."

Fear. "I'm scared that I'll get hurt. I'm scared I won't be good enough. I'm scared that once my partner really knows me, he'll leave. I'm scared to be vulnerable. I'm scared to show him my heart. I'm scared to really, really let him in without having a wall up. I'm scared. I'm scared. I'm scared. I'm scared."

Self. "Thank you. I know. Tell me more."

There is tremendous healing power in naming the different parts of yourself and allowing them to have a voice. When you dialogue, you're training your brain to move toward the parts of you that you normally, habitually want to hide away and deny. This is how you learn to gain mastery over your thoughts and feelings instead of letting them control your life and using them as the litmus test for your decision-making process. You make room for all thoughts and feelings, bathing them in the wash of acceptance, and then you connect to something deeper inside you: a space between your thoughts and beneath your feelings; your calm parent; your wise self. The more you unhook from the stories and sit in the seat of Self, the less anxiety will control your life. For countless people, journaling, when practiced daily, is the gateway to inner freedom.

RECOMMENDATIONS FOR FURTHER LEARNING

Sheryl's Online Courses

"Trust Yourself: A 30-Day Program to Help You Overcome Your Fear of Failure, Caring What Others Think, Perfectionism, Difficulty Making Decisions, and Self-Doubt" to deepen your work around learning to trust and love yourself: conscious-transitions.com/trust-yourself-a-30-day-program-to-help-you-overcome-your-fear-of-failure-caring-what-others-think-perfectionism-difficulty-making-decisions-and-self-doubt/.

"Break Free from Relationship Anxiety E-Course" if you're struggling with relationship anxiety: conscious-transitions.com/break-free-from-relationship-anxiety-e-course/.

"Grace Through Uncertainty: A 30-Day Course to Become More Comfortable with the Fear of Loss by Falling in Love with Life" to become more comfortable with uncertainty: conscious-transitions.com/grace-through-uncertainty-a-30-day-course-to-become-more-comfortable-with-the-fear-of-loss-by-falling-in-love-with-life/.

To see all of my courses, visit conscious-transitions.com/courses.

Books

Aron, Elaine. *The Highly Sensitive Person: How to Thrive When the World Overwhelms You*. New York: Three Rivers Press, 1999.

Bloom, Linda, and Charlie Bloom. *101 Things I Wish I Knew When I Got Married: Simple Lessons to Make Love Last*. Novato, CA: New World Library, 2010.

Bridges, William. *The Way of Transition: Embracing Life's Most Difficult Moments*. Cambridge, MA: Perseus Books, 2001. (I loved this one more than the original.)

Bridges, William. *Transitions: Making Sense of Life's Changes,* 2nd ed. Cambridge, MA: Da Capo Press, 2004.

Cain, Susan. *Quiet: The Power of Introverts in a World that Can't Stop Talking.* New York: Random House, 2013.

Dweck, Carol. *Mindset: The New Psychology of Success.* New York: Random House, 2006.

Hollis, James. *The Middle Passage: From Misery to Meaning in Midlife.* Toronto: Inner City Books, 1993.

Johnson, Robert. *Inner Work: Using Dreams and Active Imagination for Personal Growth.* New York: HarperOne, 2009.

Johnson, Robert. *We: Understanding the Psychology of Romantic Love.* New York: Harper, 2013.

Kerrigan, Kate. *Recipes for a Perfect Marriage.* London: Macmillan, 2016.

Kidd, Sue Monk. *When the Heart Waits: Spiritual Direction for Life's Sacred Questions.* San Francisco: HarperSanFrancisco, 2006.

Kornfield, Jack. *A Lamp in the Darkness: Illuminating the Path Through Difficult Times.* Boulder, CO: Sounds True, 2014.

Lindbergh, Anne Morrow. *Gift from the Sea.* New York: Pantheon, 1955.

Mooney, Jonathan. *The Short Bus: A Journey Beyond Normal.* New York: Henry Holt, 2008.

Nepo, Mark. *The Book of Awakening: Having the Life You Want by Being Present in the Life You Have.* Newburyport, MA: Conari Press, 2011.

Reznick, Charlotte. *The Power of Your Child's Imagination: How to Transform Stress and Anxiety into Joy and Success.* New York: Penguin, 2009.

Richo, David. *When Love Meets Fear: Becoming Defense-less and Resource-full.* New York: Paulist Press, 1997.

Saltz, Gail. *The Power of Different: The Link Between Disorder and Genius.* New York: Flatiron Books, 2018.

Siegel, Daniel. *Mindsight: The New Science of Personal Transformation.* New York: Bantam Books, 2011.

Taylor, Jeremy. *The Wisdom of Your Dreams: Using Dreams to Tap into Your Unconscious and Transform Your Life.* New York: Jeremy P. Tarcher/Penguin, 2009.

Weil, Andrew. *Natural Health, Natural Medicine: The Complete Guide to Wellness and Self-Care for Optimum Health.* Boston: Houghton Mifflin, 2004.

Audios

Chödrön, Pema. *When Things Fall Apart.* New York: Random House Audio, 2017.

Steindl-Rast, David. *A Grateful Heart.* Boulder, CO: Sounds True, 1992.

Woodman, Marion. *Sitting by the Well.* Corralitos, CA: Marion Woodman Foundation, 2007.

For more resources, please see "Books That Have Changed My Life" on my website: conscious-transitions.com/books-that-have-changed-my-life/.

ABOUT THE AUTHOR

Raised in Los Angeles by two psychotherapists, Sheryl Paul grew up with the language and theories of psychology stirring in her soul. From the time she was six years old, she faithfully kept a journal where she recorded her dreams, wrote poetry, and reflected on her daily experiences, including an early awareness that she would one day grow up to help people explore and navigate their inner landscapes.

In 1997, she graduated from Pacifica Graduate Institute, a program that specializes in Jungian depth psychology, with a master's degree in counseling. She later wrote her first book, *The Conscious Bride*, which explored the underbelly of the transition of getting married, and her second book, *The Conscious Bride's Wedding Planner*. She has appeared several times on *The Oprah Winfrey Show*, as well as on *Good Morning America* and other top media shows and publications around the globe. Through her blog, books, and courses, Sheryl has guided thousands of people worldwide through the terrain of anxiety.

Sheryl and her husband live on a creek in Colorado where they raise their two boys. You can learn more about her and her work through her website and blog at conscious-transitions.com.

ABOUT SOUNDS TRUE

Sounds True is a multimedia publisher whose mission is to inspire and support personal transformation and spiritual awakening. Founded in 1985 and located in Boulder, Colorado, we work with many of the leading spiritual teachers, thinkers, healers, and visionary artists of our time. We strive with every title to preserve the essential "living wisdom" of the author or artist. It is our goal to create products that not only provide information to a reader or listener, but that also embody the quality of a wisdom transmission.

For those seeking genuine transformation, Sounds True is your trusted partner. At SoundsTrue.com you will find a wealth of free resources to support your journey, including exclusive weekly audio interviews, free downloads, interactive learning tools, and other special savings on all our titles.

To learn more, please visit SoundsTrue.com/freegifts or call us toll-free at 800.333.9185.